Praise for *Life after College*

"*Life after College* offers a balanced, sensible approach to life as a young adult in America. The book is compassionate in its approach and conversational in tone as it guides readers through the transition from college student to working professional. It's about personal branding. It's about health and well-being. It's about equanimity—finding that balance between who you are and who you want to become. The narrative is accompanied by great stories of life lessons, told in an endearing way. Whereas Tori and Betsy's *Land Your Dream Career* ought to be read by every college sophomore, *Life after College* ought to be read by every college senior. It opens the door to the many joys in life that college students want to realize."

—Douglas J. Swanson, California State University, Fullerton

"Once again, Tori and Betsy have provided millennials with a practical, real, and sometimes humorous roadmap to success. The transition from college student to professional is a difficult one. *Life after College* provides tools and strategies for not only making it through this transition but also thriving during this often tumultuous time."

—Timothy M. Stearns, Coleman Foundation Chair in Entrepreneurship, executive director, Lyles Center for Innovation and Entrepreneurship, California State University, Fresno

"I found *Life after College* to be a well-organized and witty read, relevant to adults in all stages of life. The 'Story' sections, in which the authors share real-life experiences, were a nice touch. I could appreciate the authors' different experiences and journeys for each idea or lesson. Well done, Tori and Betsy."

—Edgar Blunt, co-founder of Career Pillar

Life after College

Ten Steps to Build a Life You Love

Tori Randolph Terhune
and Betsy A. Hays

Rowman & Littlefield
Lanham • Boulder • New York • Toronto • Plymouth, UK

Published by Rowman & Littlefield
4501 Forbes Boulevard, Suite 200, Lanham, Maryland 20706
www.rowman.com

10 Thornbury Road, Plymouth PL6 7PP, United Kingdom

British Library Cataloguing in Publication Information Available

Library of Congress Cataloging-in-Publication Data

Terhune, Tori Randolph.
  Life after college : ten steps to build a life you love / Tori Randolph Terhune and
Betsy A. Hays.
    pages cm
  Includes index.
  ISBN 978-1-4422-2597-8 (cloth : alk. paper) — ISBN 978-1-4422-2598-5
(electronic) 1. College graduates—Employment. 2. Career development. 3. Life skills.
4. Success. I. Hays, Betsy A. II. Title.
  HD6277.T463 2014
  650.1—dc23

                                                                2014003499

♾™ The paper used in this publication meets the minimum requirements of American
National Standard for Information Sciences—Permanence of Paper for Printed Library
Materials, ANSI/NISO Z39.48-1992.

Printed in the United States of America

CONTENTS

ACKNOWLEDGMENTS

This book is dedicated to the amazing Christy Patron, who inspired this book over lunch at the delicious Dog House Grill. Thank you, Christy!

And so many other folks to thank! Thank you to our fabulous agent, Anne Devlin, and everyone at our publisher, Rowman & Littlefield. Tori's husband, David, puppy, Koda, and kitten, Hunter; and Betsy's husband, Brad, daughters Sam and Jackie, and her faithful writing companion and dog, Max.

We'd like to thank Tori's family of editors: Carolyn Randolph, Melanie Randolph, John Randolph, Taylor Terhune, Mari Terhune, Dave Terhune, and Betsy's family, Nancy Tucker and Monica Barron.

Other amazing people who shared their support and wisdom: Jim Randolph, Jan Edwards, Roberta Asahina, Kim Mooney, Angie Tarr, Merrilee Montgomery, Megan Lerma, Reganie Smith-Love, Carson Best, Anne McClintic, and Kimberlee Peyret.

And so much thanks to those who helped specifically with chapter 2, Eric Martin, CFP, of Martin, Wardin & Eissner Financial Group (mwe financial.com); and chapter 4, Amy Brogan, EdD, certified health coach and college nutrition professor (agapenutritionandfitness.com).

Thank you! Thank you! Thank you!
Tori and Betsy

INTRODUCTION

Whether employed or not upon completing their college degree, most people experience a significant "culture shock" while transitioning from student to professional life. We know we did, and so did everyone we know. (Hence, why we wrote this book!)

As you now know, there is so much more to being a successful post-college human than getting a job. This book walks you, the recent (or not-so-recent) college graduate, through easily conquering ALL parts of this significant transition. From friends and dating to alarm clocks and getting promoted, this book provides the blueprint, including dealing with still sitting at the kids table at holiday meals, becoming a problem solver (not identifier), the magic of mentoring, key generational differences, and the millennial "validation vacuum."

We picked up where we left off with our first book, *Land Your Dream Career: Eleven Steps to Take in College* to provide you with an honest, humorous, and practical guide to thriving in postcollege life.

By writing this book together (a successful recent graduate and a more "seasoned" college professor), we are able to provide you with both real-time advice and experience-based knowledge—a combination that we hope will serve you well. At the end of each chapter we have once again included "Cheat Sheets" for either preview or review as you work your way through the book.

Enjoy!

CHAPTER ONE
TIME AND SLEEP MANAGEMENT
Betsy

One of the biggest challenges postgraduation is that your life isn't as fragmented as it has been for the last several years. As a student, you got used to rushing from work to school to your internship to your club meeting and back to school. So you would think that your time management now would be easier, but you may have found that it isn't. You may spend most of your day in one or two places, but that doesn't make distractions or temptations disappear, and those distractions can steer you away from what you should be doing. There is also that darn office candy bowl calling your name (but advice about the candy bowl is in chapter 4!).

Effective time and sleep management can help you build and protect your professional brand (the impression people have of you as a new professional). Your brand is best built by using consistent, positive behaviors that reinforce what YOU want the world to think about you (especially when you are not in the room, which is where true feelings are often revealed!). In our work, Tori and I talk to people a lot about "brand builders" and "brand killers." Brand builders are things that help you solidify your brand and accomplish your goals, and brand killers are things that harm your brand and deter you from your goals. Everything in this book can be a brand builder for you.

To get you in the proper frame of mind, here is what you need to do in order to have effective time management:

- Gain focus.
- Have a system.

- Be flexible within your structure.

- Prioritize your workload.

We'll go over each of these in depth now.

Gain Focus

There is a lot of great information out there regarding awesome time-management systems and maximizing productivity. In fact, there are actually gurus in this area, and we encourage you to check them out if you are really into this. See the notes at the end of this chapter for references and resources!

We, and just about all of the sources throughout and at the end of this chapter, share the belief that no time management system will help if you have no clue what your life goals are, or where you want your life to go. If you don't have a handle on these things, you will have no idea how you should be spending your time. So this is where we will start.

Start with the Big Picture

Right now, make some notes (electronically or with pen and paper—it doesn't matter—this whole book is customizable to YOU and how you like to do things). In these notes, jot down:

1. Words that describe your ideal life. Include roles or titles that you have now and want to have in the future (i.e., amazing friend, parent, president, accountant, swimmer, etc.).

2. Adjectives (healthy, funny, well-read, creative, etc.)

3. Very specific tasks, like a "bucket list" (i.e., travel to Italy on vacation, learn to speak Chinese, run a 10K, etc.)

Be sure that you include a healthy, heaping dose of authenticity in this exercise. These are YOUR words for your life. Not your parents' words, or your significant others' or your friends' words. They are *yours*, and this will only work if you follow directions! Make the list as long as you would like, and have fun with it! This is the time to dream BIG. There are no limits to this list.

Next, let the list sit. Leave the list alone for a day or so, and then pick it up again. Very quickly, and without thinking about it too much, cross off everything that doesn't speak to you anymore. You might have nothing to cross off, or you might have lots of things. Again, this is all about YOU. (Yay, right? We love things that are all about us!)

Look at the remaining list and start ranking things. What are the most important items on your list? As awkward as this may be, ask yourself, "At the end of my life, what do I want to make sure I am or have done from this list?" You may have "ties" here—several things as number one, and so on. That is fine. Do the best you can.

Figure in Seasons

We love the idea that our lives have seasons. You can think of this analogy using traditional seasons—spring, summer, fall, and winter—and the ebb and flow of all things in nature. Another way to think about this is to use a sports theme—every sport has a preseason, a season, a postseason (hopefully!), and an off-season before it all starts again. Think about it in whichever way is more fun for you, but focus on the idea that what we can do in the summer we can't do in the winter, and what you should focus on in the preseason is not what your priorities are in the middle of the season. This translates well with what we want you to do next with your list.

Once you have your LIFE PRIORITIES list, think about the "when" piece of it. What makes sense to work on right now? What makes sense to work on in the future? And when in the future should that be? With some luck and a bunch of fruits and vegetables, your life will be long, and you don't have to (nor can you) do everything at once. This is why you need to chunk your list into "seasons" or time periods. Some of your priorities will stay the same over time (exercising and eating healthy, for example), but many will now be housed in decades or sections of your life that you can label prekids and postkids or something like that. Perhaps your main focus right now is your professional life, and in your thirties you want to go to grad school. Or maybe now you want to travel a lot, and when you retire take up painting. Again, it is *your* life, so the order of things is up to you! We highly encourage you not to let society's typical formula for how a person's life is supposed to go dictate your timeline. YOU dictate your timeline. Please. It's the only way you can have the life *you* want.

> **Note:** Because we as humans don't know how long we will be on this earth, it is tempting to try and accomplish ALL of our LIFE PRIORITIES right now so we won't have any regrets later. This is a bad idea, because having too many priorities leads to a big mess when it comes to effective time management. It will be hard, but you have to make some tough choices here and put off some things for another time. The great thing about this, to pull in the optimism piece, is that you will always have something amazing to look forward to in each season or time period in your life!

Don't Rush

Please don't be in a hurry to get married, have babies, buy a house, and other goals. You need to go with your timeline, not the timeline of others. Rushing into these major life events because everyone around you seems to be doing them, or because you feel that you "should," is usually a big, big mistake. There are many divorces and defaulted mortgages out there to prove this point, and you don't want to be part of either of these statistics. In the year or two after I graduated from college, I went to three weddings in which the marriages ended up lasting six months, which was obviously very hard on those involved. If you ask any of these folks if they saw it coming, the honest ones would say yes. Don't just do something because it's the "typical" next step. Do it because you want to and your gut tells you it's time.

> **Note from Tori:** This is so true! My parents were married right out of college, and all of their friends who were married around the same time are now divorced (including my godparents). In my personal life, I know that my best friend, my husband, and I all broke up with our long-term relationships within a year of graduating from college. And we were all close to engagement (in fact, my friend was proposed to before she broke it off!). When you graduate you will go through a lot of personal growth, and you'll be surprised to find that you may not deal with these life changes the same way as your significant other. Give yourself time to grow, and if your relationship can last through the first few years after college, you'll be much more equipped to handle getting married (and we'll talk more about these relationships in chapter 5!).

Get Rid of the Things That Don't Match

Now that your LIFE PRIORITIES have been identified and you've organized them into the chunks of time in which you want to focus on them, take a look at your current life. Write down the main things you spend your time doing, and match these things with your current list of LIFE PRIORITIES. You will most likely find some disconnects. (We all do—don't worry!) There are things that you spend time doing that don't help you work toward the life you want. As best as you can, cross these things off your to-do list. This may mean you stop being a member of a club, or you see some people in your life less frequently (or not at all). And, again, this exercise might be hard, but it is so worth it! We can't even describe how amazing things are when your LIFE PRIORITIES list and your to-do list match up.

Do a Reality Check

You might find that there are some things on your LIFE PRIORI-TIES list that, if you really think about them, might be considered "long shots" or "unrealistic." Now is the time to consider whether or not those things should stay on your list. If they are important to you, and/or give your life purpose, and/or you can't imagine life without them—obviously keep them. But if these things cause you stress, or you believe that they aren't really achievable given how your life is headed, perhaps it's time to delete them, or move them to a different list (i.e., the goals-to-evaluate-when-I-turn-thirty list). Just about all of us grow up wanting to be sports or rock stars or famous artists or inventors. And if that is more important to you than breathing, please, continue the quest. But if it isn't, or you have an injury, lack of talent, or life circumstances that make these ideas nearly impossible, please move on. If you move ahead and go for it, make sure you move with purpose and passion!

Create the Little Picture

Once you have dumped the things, people, organizations, tasks, and more that don't have anything to do with the life you want, what you will have left is your list of want-to-dos, obligations you can't get out of, and your work. This list is what you should focus on, and this is the list that all invitations for meetings, projects, appointments, and events should be measured against. When someone asks you to do something, make sure it fits your current list of LIFE PRIORITIES. If it does AND you have time to do it without sacrificing sleep or sanity, say yes. If not, say no thank you. If you really want to do this particular thing at some point but right now you don't have time, write it down and see if you do have time in a few weeks or months.

Let the Little Steps Add Up

You are probably familiar with this idea as it relates to money and interest (more about this in chapter 2!), but it doesn't just work its magic there. This idea, also called the compounding effect, can get you just about everything you want. The key: work toward each of your goals in small increments on most days. Want to write a book? Write for a period of time most days. Want to lose weight? Exercise most days. Want to master Italian? Work on it most days. Want to read two books a week? Read some at lunchtime or every night before you go to sleep.

Life success is not about perfection; it's about consistency. All of the little things you spend time on each day add up to big results. Many of us waste time waiting for large chunks of time to magically appear in our day in order to get our big projects done, and this just doesn't happen. It's the few minutes a day on the things that are important that get the jobs done. Start using the compounding effect today. Again, you'll have to make choices (maybe less TV or video games or social media or sleeping), but it will be worth it!

Note: After I wrote this chapter I found a book about this very topic, *The Compound Effect* by Darren Hardy. I read it, of course, and loved it! (And I think you should read it, too, if you like this idea as much as we do.)

Check in Regularly

Make sure you set up appointments with yourself to check in regularly with your LIFE PRIORITIES list to make sure things are still accurate. For example, you may have initially thought that you wanted to train for a 10K, but when you joined the gym, you discovered that swimming is more your thing. If that's the case, cross the 10K off your list—it's no longer what YOU want to do. As most time management gurus advocate (and we agree), schedule check-ins daily, weekly, monthly, and semiannually. Here are some ideas to help you through your check-ins.

Daily

At the end of each day, spend a few minutes organizing for tomorrow. Think about:

- what you need to bring to work or wherever you are going the next day (lunch, gym clothes, library book, etc.)

- what you need to take out of the freezer for dinner

- what time you should get up

- what calls you can make during commute time (via a headset, of course—we want you to drive safely!)

- other things that can help your tomorrow go more smoothly

Weekly

On the same day each week, spend a few minutes and do the following:

- Set up your to-do list for next week, including prepping for and attending the appointments on your calendar.

- Send emails or text messages confirming all of your appointments for next week. (Just doing this alone saves you so much time and energy by eliminating meetings that people "forgot" about and clears up any confusion on times or dates.)

- Ponder the prior week. What went well? What didn't go so well? How could you have planned or organized your time better? Were there priorities that were neglected? Do some priorities need to be adjusted?

Monthly

Once a month, spend a little more time pondering the items we asked you to ponder above. Think strategically regarding how you could make your actual life match closer with your ideal life. What changes do you have to make? How can you fit those changes into your life on a daily or weekly basis?

Semiannually

Twice a year, really sit and think about your life. Look at your list of LIFE PRIORITIES, and see if anything has changed. Is there something that you initially thought you wanted to wait to do that now feels more urgent? Is there something you thought was important right now that can wait? Or maybe even not get done at all?

Tip: One way to make sure that your life is in sync with your LIFE PRIORITIES is to keep a journal. Armen, one of the most inspiring women we know and also an author and public relations professional, suggests to her mentees that they keep a journal to log those tasks and activities that bring them joy and a sense of true accomplishment and satisfaction. This will help you tremendously when you want to hone in on the kind of work you are "meant to do" (or perhaps even destined to do!) and what work leaves you unfulfilled.

Evenings, Weekends, and Days Off

We encourage you to also really think about how you choose to spend your weekends and days off. There is no wrong answer, of course, but those who enjoy their evenings, weekends, and days off are those that are thoughtful about them ahead of time. Don't think that you need hard-and-fast rules that apply to every evening, weekend, or day off. All we ask is that you think about it, and, if it's appropriate, make a plan. Those who "wing it" tend to not feel satisfied or recharged with their time off. Now, this is not to say that you should never choose to "do nothing" with any of your free time. Obviously, this choice is one that is important to many in order to recharge. The point is, you should "choose" to do nothing. And enjoy it. And not feel guilty about it.

If you feel you waste a lot of time when you are not working, make a plan to change. Allow yourself a chunk of time to "waste," if you'd like, and then figure out what you'd like to do in order to feel that you have done what YOU wanted with your time.

Please do not underestimate the importance of recharging your batteries. It is so easy to power through it, especially when you are younger and have a lot of energy (or even if you are older and have a lot of energy!).

A Story

Literally an hour before I did the final edit of this chapter, I was talking to my husband about our plans for the day. It was a Saturday, and it had been an extremely busy week (including a work event the night before that kept me out late), and we had a lot going on with the kids and errands—typical Saturday stuff. The evening plans were a little complex, including feeding my daughter and her friends before a dance, taking my daughter and her friends to a dance, meeting my husband and other daughter at a football game, and then leaving the game early to pick up the kids from the dance. My husband asked me, "Are you sure you want to do all of that?" I replied, "It'll be fine. I have an amazing amount of energy." He then reminded me that while he didn't doubt that I did, he also didn't want me to be miserable. I decided to stay home from the football game, focus on getting the kids to and from the dance, and in between watch a movie (with my faithful movie companion and dog, Max). My batteries were able to recharge a bit, and I was grateful I didn't choose to "power through" just because I could.

Have a System (Compatible with Your Life)

Let's take this idea of compatibility first. Any system you create will fail if it isn't compatible with your life. If you never use a pen, don't create a paper-based system. If you feel upset if you run out of sticky notes, then a fully electronic system is not for you. And, to be honest, we don't think that an either fully electronic or fully paper-based system is the best route for anyone. We love hybrid systems, because they flex, and we think that flexing is the key to success in everything. Our hybrid systems are primarily electronic.

I use Evernote.com for my to-do lists, making them available on my laptop and my mobile devices. However, I also never go anywhere without pen and paper, as I still enjoy writing things down as I think of them without having to type anything in. I have a specific place I keep these notes, and I have a routine to sync them with my electronic to-do list the very next time I am on my computer. This works for me, but it might not work for you, and that is OK, as long as you (a) have a system and (b) it is compatible with your life.

Tori uses OneNote on her tablet for her LIFE PRIORITIES and to-do lists, and she carries her tablet everywhere. She also emails herself on her smartphone if she needs to make a quick note. Tori schedules everything on her Google calendar that she can access anywhere on any device, but she also carries a planner so she can easily see all of her meetings for the week and month at a glance (something that isn't easy to do on her phone calendar), plus she loves to cross things off! On her Google calendar she created a different calendar for every aspect of her life (each client, personal, writing, appointments, etc.) and gave them each a different color so she can easily see where her time is going each week by color.

Calendars

Calendars are awesome, but we probably don't have to tell you that. What we do want to tell you, however, is the importance of using them consistently. Use a calendar that syncs with both your computer and your smartphone so you can include appointments in your calendar the minute you schedule them and nothing falls through the cracks. *Make a rule that you never commit to anything without checking your calendar.* This saves all kinds of time and drama (and also gives you time to think of an "out" if you decide that you really don't want to do that thing anyway!). These days with our mobile lives, you need to have your calendar with you at all times, so having it on your phone or in your pocket/purse is essential.

To-Do List(s)

We find that most people have so much going on that they can really only focus on their current week's responsibilities, so that's what we actually do—and what we recommend—as long as you are keeping tabs on what is happening the next week, month, and more. While your focus must be in the present, you must always have some of your attention (at least a little bit each day) focused on what's coming up so you can gather information or ideas that will help you prepare.

Please, please, please get in the habit of writing everything down. Establish this habit now, while your memory works beautifully, and you'll be exponentially happier later when your memory doesn't work as well. (This really does happen to all of us!) Writing down everything does the obvious—it allows nothing to fall through cracks via forgetting—but it also helps you by making sure you only have to think of things once, so your very powerful brain can use its energy on things other than remembering, such as problem-solving and creativity (MUCH better uses of its magic!). Let your lists take care of the remembering.

Most people find it works best if they have several lists, but how you organize those lists is up to you. You may want to have a work list and a home list, or you may like all of your items on one list. You might want a list for each day, and then another list for the next week and the next month so you can keep track of things that you want to do but aren't priorities right now. You may also want to have other lists for each project that have more detail.

However you organize your list, make sure that your daily lists are actually quite small, or maybe listed by levels. Realistically, you should have very few "must do" tasks, or things that HAVE TO be done today. Most of our lists are longer than they need to be because we always think we can get more done than we can, and this unrealistic "to-do listing" is not how you set yourself up for success. Having a to-do list that is too long leaves you feeling either constantly overwhelmed (a recipe for procrastination) and/or like you fail every day (does THAT sound like a good idea?).

So pick the MOST important things that you have to accomplish, list those first, do those first, and then you can perhaps fit in a few more "it would be lovely if these things happened today" items, and *always feel a sense of accomplishment*. How does that sound? We think having a daily sense of accomplishment sounds pretty good. Remember the compounding effect: Small and regular steps toward all goals are how you actually accomplish things.

Figure the When

When you do the things on your to-do list is almost as important as *what* is on your list. We all have times during the day that are more productive than others. Some of us are early risers (me), and some of us are amazing at working long into the night (Tori). Know yourself, and know when you should work on your "thinking" tasks, when you should work on your "brainless" tasks, and when you should not really work on anything because working at this time is slow, unproductive, and would be better used for recharging activities such as exercise or sleep.

Also keep in mind, and be honest about, your routines. For example, if you tend to unwind after a long day with a glass of wine (or two) with dinner (at home and not driving!), then you're much less likely to be active or energized afterward, so don't plan on completing an active or energizing activity. For example, if this is you, don't schedule a trip to the gym after dinner! It's probably not going to happen, and that's OK. Just figure out a better time to work out.

Have Accountability

A time-management system often works well when there is accountability involved. You can do this internally, keeping track of the days that you accomplish your most important items and rewarding yourself for your success with small treats that are meaningful to you. Or, you can do this externally, by engaging an "accountability partner" who you report your progress to on a daily or weekly basis. You can use internal accountability for some things and external for others—whatever formula works best for you. For the projects we work on together, Tori and I keep each other accountable by having very specific project lists and deadlines and weekly meetings where each of us are expected to have our work accomplished. Are we always perfect? No, but knowing that someone else is expecting you to have your stuff done, and you know that he/she will have his/her stuff done, certainly makes you work harder and try to avoid excuses.

Delete Excuses

In fact, let's talk about excuses a little bit here. Sure, things come up and life happens, but today and this next week try to pay attention to when you are thinking about giving someone an excuse for why something didn't get done. Usually we need excuses when we have messed up—procrastinated, didn't give ourselves time to do the project or task, or were just plain lazy or distracted. The next time you think about giving someone an excuse, stop yourself. And don't. Push through. Get whatever it is done, and toss that excuse (and the brand killing that goes with it!) into your metaphoric trash can. If you do this often enough, you will find yourself using less and less excuses.

On a related note, don't use being "busy" as a badge of honor—because quite frankly, it isn't. EVERYONE is busy, so you being busy does NOT make you special, or even make you stand out. Think about it. People who talk all the time about how busy they are tend to be extremely annoying (not a brand builder!). And even if you really are busier than everyone else, no one really cares (except perhaps your mom), and often those types of conversations tend to morph into a "who is busier?" metaphoric "pissing contest" (sorry for the blunt language!). These conversations never lead to a winner, or anything positive for that matter.

What can make you stand out, however, is being able to manage your business with a calm persona. This is most certainly brand-building behavior! Instead of explaining how busy you are and why you didn't get something done, get it done, and let people know how effectively you manage your time (even though you are so busy!).

Set Time Limits

Most people don't have unlimited time to work on their projects, and we are assuming that you are no different. So use this to your advantage. Look at your list of tasks for today, and make a plan for how much time you need/want to spend on each of them. Then use a timer to track yourself so you are consistently staying on track. Allow for some wiggle room, of course (e.g., maybe a five-to-ten-minute break between new projects so you can pop in and check email to make sure the day's priorities are still the same). Use an online timer, an inexpensive actual timer that you hold in your hand, or the timer on your phone. The idea is to stop clock watching or worrying about time. We want you to focus on the work that you are doing, and that is it!

> **Tip:** I use the free website www.online-stopwatch.com to track my time while I work.

For each task, give yourself a minimum and maximum amount of time. This flexibility is important, because minimums give you an "out" if things aren't flowing well, and maximums give you some extra time to spend on something if you are really on a roll (or don't want to move to your next task quite yet!). Usually we need both of these tools at our disposal.

Don't forget to schedule breaks in between your timed activities. Most often five to ten minutes is best, so you can have a break but not get completely caught up in something else. Give yourself "rules" for your breaks (i.e., you must get up, stretch, walk around, get a drink of water, etc.). DO NOT sit at your desk for your entire break time. This doesn't help you become "fresh" for your next task. The physical act of standing up and/or walking around will probably trigger some creative thinking, which we always welcome, right?

Chunk It

When you've got a big project, it often helps to chunk it into smaller pieces. And make the chunks easy to accomplish so you won't procrastinate. This is a much better plan than waiting for huge chunks of time to appear in your calendar. As we all know, this doesn't just happen! Remember the old adage, "How do you eat an elephant? One bite at a time." Chunking will help you avoid procrastination and actually make progress. You may want to chunk all of your goals—both personal and professional. For example, if you want to learn Japanese, start by learning a few words a day for a month or so, and then buy an audiobook, then take an online or in-person class, and then maybe even schedule a trip to Japan. You get the idea. Small, easy-to-implement steps are the fastest path to accomplishing your goals. It's just like the story about the tortoise and the hare—slow and steady wins the race.

Manage Email and All Other Forms of Electronic Messaging

Most of us have a love-hate relationship with email, and we are right there with you. But it is a reality of modern life, and we need to make sure that we control it—not the other way around. This goes for ALL types of electronic messaging. We no longer differentiate between Twitter or Facebook messages and email. If someone reaches out to us electronically, they need a response, and we need a plan! The fact that we can get all of this on our phones makes it even more important for us to manage it well, as we've all had days when all we do is send and receive messages and our to-do list remains untouched. *This is NOT what the day of a successful person looks like.*

To manage electronic messages (email, social media, etc.):

1. Ditch automatic notifications. Make it so you have to go into your email inbox or Facebook app in order to see if there is anything new. Just like you decide when to go to your actual physical mailbox, YOU decide when to visit your virtual inboxes, not the other way around. Your devices should work for you. You should not be at their beck and call.

2. Select specific times each day to check messages. Perhaps morning and afternoon will work, or maybe morning, early afternoon, and evening—whenever it works best for you. Choose times when you can actually sit down at your computer or tablet and process your messages. If you must check email and other messages from your phone, do so infrequently and only when necessary, and only when you can actually spend time processing some of it. Also, consider at least not checking email most of the weekend, and perhaps spend an hour or so on Sunday processing so you can hit the ground running on Monday morning.

3. Consider having "standard" or "canned" email responses to common questions or emails you get, if this fits with your job/ life. We have many of these that we keep and cut and paste when needed, saving lots of time and energy. Gmail has its own feature, called "canned responses," that you can use if you use that email system. I also use Evernote for this purpose, with a note for each of my classes and projects that has language I can cut and paste for common questions and requests.

4. When you do check email and other messages, spend the time and effort to finish as many conversations as you can, or at least move them all forward. When you sit down to deal with all of it (now just a few times each day), move everything forward at least one step. This means answer it, file it, delete it, or put it

on your to-do list for later. Play around and develop a system that works for you. Email folders are one of the greatest gifts we have in the modern era. Below I have a list of the email folders that I use to process my emails. Again, you may want to do something differently, which is fine, but you should do something with your email so your inbox is constantly empty at the end of your email-processing sessions. Notice many of them start with "A" so they live at the top of the email folder list for quick access.

- Action NOW (things to deal with before finishing the day).

- Action Tomorrow (semiurgent things that can't be answered quickly during the email-processing session).

- Action Pending (waiting to hear back from others and want to make sure they get handled, so keep this folder as a reminder to follow-up if needed).

- Action This Week (things that need to get done this week but are not urgent, and they can't be answered quickly during the email-processing session).

- Action Next Week (things that can wait).

- Action to Read This Week (self-explanatory).

- Action HOME (emails that need to be dealt with when not working).

- A folder for each course I teach and each project that I am working on, where I can file emails that I might need to forward or access again or refer to later for those projects. These emails do not need action or a response.

5. Use your email folders to get things done. When you sit down to work, don't start with your inbox. Start with wherever you put your urgent emails, work on those, get them done, and then process your inbox until it is empty (or at least close). Fewer things (or nothing) will fall through the cracks, and your inbox will be empty often. Sounds good, right?

Manage Social Media

Just like email and other electronic messages, social media can consume your life if you are not careful. Regardless of whether or not you are allowed to engage in social media at work, whenever you engage in it, social media has the potential to keep you from the things that are really important to you (as defined above).

So how do you keep social media in its proper place in your life? See above. Turn off notifications; check it a few times a day. Get in, engage, post, and get out. Before you post, ask yourself, "Does this help me build my brand and work toward accomplishing my goals?" If yes, post it. If no, delete. This makes using social media pretty easy.

> **Note:** Another way to decide what to post is to give yourself a litmus test. I never post anything that I wouldn't say in front of my students. Tori has three people whom she keeps in mind when posting to social media. If it wouldn't make sense to these people, would offend these people, or doesn't build her brand to these people, she doesn't post it. These three people include a mentor, a relative, and a role model. Litmus tests make things SO EASY, and we are big fans of that!

Be Mindful of Opportunity Costs

Everything that you do that does not advance one of your LIFE PRIORITIES is an opportunity cost. It is costing you time (and maybe even money) that might be better spent moving you forward toward what you want to become and what you want to accomplish. Obviously, this idea applies to social media for many of us, but it also applies to other time-consuming things as well, like TV, so just be conscious of the time you are spending. And make sure it is helping you and not harming you as you set yourself up for success.

Be Flexible within Your Structure

Now that we have worked with you on building a system that fits with your life, we want to encourage you to not be so tied to it that you miss opportunities that come up each and every day. Build in flexibility as much as possible, so you can pivot and adjust and change course if necessary.

After you accomplish each major task for the day (remember these are the things you are going to do first before you can get interrupted with other people's priorities or things that come up and require your attention . . . or you just run out of steam), take a deep breath and look at your next item on your to-do list. Ask yourself: is this STILL the best use of the next chunk of my time? If it is—do it! If not, adjust.

Prioritize Your Workload

One of the best ways to prioritize your workload is to dance close to the big rocks near your revenue line. While at first this probably makes no sense, just go with us for a minute. This is a combination of two ideas that we love.

As mentioned at the end of this chapter, one of our favorite gurus is Julie Morgenstern, and in her book, *Never Check E-Mail in the Morning*, she has a chapter about dancing close to the revenue line. What she means is that our time should always be spent working closely toward the things that have the most value for us. At work, these are things that bring in revenue for our company (pitching clients, creating products, research-ing sales leads, etc.). In our nonwork lives, these are things that make us physically and emotionally healthier and strengthen our relationships. Sometimes, however, we get caught up in the "other stuff" because it is either easier or more interesting or less stressful. When we stick close to what really matters, and always keep our "revenue lines" in view, we know our time will be well spent.

The other piece of this—the big rocks—is from a frequently for-warded email story that you may have heard about. A speaker had a big jar and a bunch of big rocks, some sand, and small pebbles. He asked a mem-ber of the audience to fill the jar, first with the sand and small pebbles and then with the big rocks. As you might imagine, once the sand and small pebbles went into the jar, the big rocks didn't all fit. Then he asked them to fill the jar again, first with the big rocks and then the sand and small pebbles. This, of course, worked fine, as the sand and small pebbles filled in the spaces in the jar around the big rocks. This is a metaphor for our lives. If we don't take care of the big rocks (our LIFE PRIORITIES) first, we won't have room for them in our lives, as our lives will be spent on the sand and pebbles (the small things that don't matter as much).

So we have combined these two ideas in one, and we encourage you to dance close to the big rocks near your revenue line. If you do this, even most days, you will be extremely successful.

Ask for Help

Another great way to prioritize your workload is to ask those that are supervising you for help. When you are given a task, ask about its importance relative to the other tasks you have to do so you know which things have priority over others. Also, if you are unclear, ask questions regarding what a great job on this assignment would look like. If you and your supervisor have the same end goals in mind, you will both be happier with the results, and you won't waste time on unimportant things. You will put the appropriate amount of effort into your tasks and assignments, focusing on the areas you (and your supervisor) acknowledge as the most important. There are times when acceptable is your standard, not perfection. And there are times when perfection is what's needed. Knowing the difference can be the key to your time management success.

Something else to help you here, especially if your boss or supervisor is unavailable and you are feeling overwhelmed with your tasks at work, is to consider what has the most impact to the bottom line of your organization. Remember to "dance close to the big rocks near the revenue line." What on your list will have the most impact on your company still thriving tomorrow? This should always be at the top of your to-do list!

Other Good Time Management Tips

- Have inventory lists for things you typically buy at the grocery store and other places that you frequently shop (for us it is Target). This way, you can check your inventory (what you have in your house or apartment) and then have an accurate list of what you really need. You won't forget anything, and you won't run out as you will always be looking at how much shampoo you have left, for example.

- Only grocery shop once a week. Make menus and plan out your week so you'll only have to shop once. Endless trips to the store are among our biggest time wasters.

- Buy more than one of a cool gift that you find. If you see something that more than one person in your life might want, and you can afford it, buy more than one. This saves time shopping later. Keep an inventory, however, so you don't forget you already bought Mom's birthday gift!

- If you are one that sends cards in the mail, buy them in bulk so you always have one available and don't have to rush to the store or the mall. Do the same for stamps. You should never be without a few stamps (forever stamps are great for this purpose as they can be used regardless of postage cost changes).

- Group your errands geographically. My family calls this "trip-linking" (something I read in a magazine about energy conservation—and less trips = less gas!). I try to never leave the house for just one thing, and I try to do all of my errands on the way to work or on the way home (or if I'm out for lunch). We talk about this so often at my house that instead of asking me to take them somewhere, my kids ask me, "When is the next time we will be near (where they want to go)?" They know that their odds of getting their way increase if we will be near their desired location already.

Sleep Management

In college, you may have had a regular sleep cycle, but our guess is that you didn't. You may have also experienced days when you existed on very little sleep (remember those all-nighters?). Because of your class and work schedules, your days probably were very different from each other, or at least your Monday/Wednesday/Fridays were different from your Tuesday/Thursdays, and as a result, your sleep routine ebbed and flowed. Also, we are guessing that you didn't schedule very many 8 a.m. classes (unless it was absolutely necessary), and getting up early was probably not something you did regularly.

Regardless of how accurately or inaccurately the paragraph above describes you, now is the time to get your sleep life together. Now, in your postcollege life, most of your weekdays have a similar schedule, and being places before 9 a.m. (or even 8 a.m.) is something you are expected to do on a regular basis. If you wake up every day rested and ready to go, great! If not, read on. . . .

Establish a Routine (with Some Flexibility)

Are you sensing a theme yet? We STRONGLY advocate having routines and systems to manage your life, but always include flexibility as well. Have a routine in the morning and at night to help your body get into a rhythm. This rhythm piece is key to your success. Your routines should make sense to you (and maybe ONLY you), but try to have them not include time on electronic devices. They tend to keep you awake longer than you want to be at night, and they tend to distract heavily while you are trying to get ready in the morning. Have the last thirty minutes and the first sixty minutes of your day be "device-free," and that will probably be most of what you need to do. Include things you enjoy in your routines. For example, your morning routine could include reading the paper, making a healthy breakfast, drinking coffee on your patio, exercising, and other activities. Your evening routine could include reading a good book, taking a bath or shower, stretching, drinking hot tea, and other things.

People that go to bed at the same time and get up at the same time most days tend to do better with sleep (and frankly—life in general). Never in your life has this been easier with your new reasonable, consistent routine! Take advantage of this. Try it for two weeks and watch your body adjust.

If your life feels a little (or a lot) out of control, you'll find that these simple start-of-day and end-of-day routines will quickly bring needed order to your life. They will also give you more mental energy to face all of the exciting things you have to do!

Most of us with "issues" getting out of bed tend to have crazy, hectic mornings if we don't do some of our morning to-do items at night. If you are that person, pack your lunch, pick out your outfit, pull out your exercise clothes if your morning routine includes the gym, think about what you'll have for breakfast, set the coffee pot up in advance, and more. This will help you sleep because you'll probably be less anxious about the morning. You know that you have set yourself up for success, so you can relax and enjoy sleeping!

Use an Actual Alarm Clock—Not Your Phone

In fact, we recommend that you let your phone "sleep" in another room. It removes all temptation, and you won't roll over and start playing with it if you can't sleep—prolonging your insomnia. It doesn't have to be an expensive one, just one that works. If you are one that loves to hit the snooze button, put the alarm clock on the other side of the room so you have to get up and turn it off. This might not prevent you from ever hitting the snooze, but it will probably prevent you from hitting it several times.

Set Your Heater to Go on Automatically

In the winter, sometimes it is hard to get out of bed because it is cold, and your warm, cozy comforter is so fabulous. We get it, so, if possible, we advise you to set up your heater to go on a few minutes before your alarm clock goes off so your place will have the chill taken off before you get up—making it easier for you to do so!

So now you are on your way to beautiful time and sleep management! Please remember our mantra of customizing—use the things in this chapter that make the most sense to you, and small steps are certainly OK. You want to move forward toward the life you want, right? As long as you are moving in the right direction, the speed becomes much less important!

CHEAT SHEET

- Time management

- Gain focus
  - Start with the big picture
  - Figure in seasons
  - Don't rush
  - Get rid of the things that don't match
  - Do a reality check
  - Create the little picture
  - Let the little steps add up
  - Check in regularly
  - Evenings, weekends, and days off

- Have a system (compatible with your life)
  - Calendars
  - To-do lists
  - Figure the when
  - Have accountability
  - Delete excuses
  - Set time limits
  - Chunk it
  - Manage email and all other forms of electronic messaging
  - Manage social media
  - Be mindful of opportunity costs

- Be flexible within your structure

- Prioritize your workload
  - Ask for help

- Other good time management tips

- Sleep management
  - Establish a routine (with some flexibility)
  - Use an actual alarm clock—not your phone
  - Set your heater to go on automatically

References and Resources

Allen, David. *Getting Things Done: The Art of Stress-Free Productivity*. New York: Penguin Books, 2003. (Note: We have not read this book, but it is referenced so often as the "bible" of productivity that it deserves mention just for that reason alone!)

Evernote.com (my favorite productivity tool).

Ferriss, Tim. *The 4-Hour Workweek*. New York: Crown, 2009.

Forster, Mark. *Get Everything Done: And Still Find Time to Play*. London: Hodder Headline, 2000.

Hardy, Darren. *The Compound Effect*. Philadelphia: Vanguard Press, 2010.

Lifehack.org. www.Lifehack.org (one of the most amazing blogs EVER).

Morgenstern, Julie. *Never Check E-Mail in the Morning*. New York: Fireside, 2004.

HUGE shout-outs to all of these folks for being our heroes!

MONEY, BENEFITS, TAXES, AND INSURANCE
Tori

W hen I first graduated from college I put a deposit on an apartment that I loved. It was a little out of my price range, but I decided I would just "figure it out later." As time went on, I did have to figure it out to make sure I had enough to pay taxes, pay my bills on time, and afford to spend on things I wanted.

The problem for me was that I didn't have a "normal" job. In fact, following a summer internship after my freshman year of college where I was a full-time corporate intern, I knew the "9-to-5" office life wasn't for me. My first job out of college was a work-from-home situation, and since then I have been self-employed, contracting out full time to other companies so that I can have control over my time and workspace. It sounds like fun, right? It is, except for when tax time rolls around. And retirement planning. And insurance. And really anything that has anything to do with finances.

I'll admit it. I've never been great with finances. While I did well in math class and I can add pretty quickly in my head, when it comes to spreadsheets, budgets, and balancing, my head starts to swim. You may be wondering, *so why I am I learning this from you?* Stick with me. I'm a work in progress, and I want to share my struggles and successes, as well as the struggles and successes of other recent graduates. Not only have I learned a lot from personal experience, but I sought out expert advice for this chapter; I sat down with my financial planner, Eric P. Martin, CFP (www.mwefinancial.com), to interview him (and "suck everything out of his brain" as Betsy likes to say). I was thrilled about everything he was willing to share, and I think you will be, too.

First, I'll start with a quick tip to use as you graduate from college. If you are reading this and are still in school, get ready for this huge transition. Try to cancel all recurring financial commitments, even if you know you have a job and can afford it. Leading up to graduation you may have grants or loans, an allowance from your parents, or a cheaper living situation that you occasionally overlook when planning ahead for the future. Consider canceling anything with a recurring monthly charge so that you can decide what is truly a priority in your new budget. START FRESH as much as you can.

A Story

My sister CJ graduated from college recently. She knew she had a job postgraduation, and so she wasn't worried about paying her normal bills or changing her lifestyle. It wasn't until she graduated and moved out on her own that she realized everything that she had to budget for. Mom and Dad had paid for her gas and cell phone, had given her an allowance, and paid for housing. While she knew she'd have to start paying rent, the gas and phone cost increase, combined with not having an allowance, was a bit of a shock to her lifestyle. Not to mention, she had a personal physical trainer whom she met with several times a week. And then, to make matters worse, she found out she owed a $900 housing security deposit that she had to pay in four days.

As big sister, and someone who had lived through this transition already, I talked to her about all these financial changes and how it's all a part of growing up. The $900 seemed like a huge deal right after graduation, but when we broke down her budget we knew she would be fine. She pulled the cash out of her credit card and only needed to go out a few times less per month to pay it off and stay debt-free.

Create Your Blueprint with the End in Mind

After you've graduated and, hopefully, been able to budget for your rent and basic living expenditures, you need to get your blueprint ready. Your blueprint will help you with your budget and lifestyle, as well as help you plan for the future and be comfortable later in your life. While it may seem far away right now, the earlier you get started, the easier it will be for you to save for your future. Your blueprint will make it easy, and, if you follow it, will keep you financially stable.

There are five pieces you need for your blueprint to keep you successful with your financial plan.

Live Below Your Income

This is first and most important. Do not think that you can spend exactly what you make every month and be financially stable. You must live as if you make less than you really do. This helps you to spend better, save better, and ultimately live better. Your general rule of thumb should be that your living expenses should only account for half of your paycheck. You want the extra money for other expenditures, car or home repairs, emergency funds, and savings.

Sit down for a moment and take an inventory of everything you spend and then how much you will make from your job; see if you need to make any cuts. If you do, don't worry. It may be a temporary cut that you have to make while building up your paycheck and asking for raises until you can get to the standard of living that you want. Remember that you are young! As a twenty-something you really shouldn't be able to afford everything you want on your own. Start saving and planning for the future you want so you can enjoy it when you are able to.

A Story

Figuring out your budget is very important, but you also have to know yourself and know what you like to spend your money on so you can set yourself up for successful budgeting. If you budget $100 per month for shoes, that's great. But if you can't stick to that and spend $200 on shoes every month, your budget isn't working. A story I love to share is from my parents when they first graduated from college and got married. My mom was still trying to get her first job, so my dad put them both on a very strict budget. My mom grew up with a credit card that was paid by her parents, and she never had to worry about money in her account or budgeting. When my dad put her on a budget of $100 per week, she went over in the first week. My dad was understanding and told her that it would just come out of the next week. That made sense, until she spent more than $100 the next week as well. At the end of the first month, she had spent several hundred dollars over her budget, and she knew this system wasn't going to work for her. Fortunately, she soon found a job, established a separate checking account, and created and stuck to her own budget.

Pay Off Your Credit Cards Every Month

This should be a no-brainer, but there are those who have multiple credit cards and don't think that it is a big deal to carry debt over for a few months. Others think that it actually helps your credit score to have a balance carry over; this is NOT the case! You want to pay your credit card off every month and keep the amount of cards you have to a minimum. Let me give you a few scenarios in which paying off your credit card can help you.

- When you don't pay off your credit card every month, you are left with paying interest, or extra charges based on a percentage of what you owe, to the credit card company. Not only does this mean you are losing this money, but imagine what you could do if you put the money you would be paying as interest into a savings account and let it gain interest for you instead. You want to keep and save your money, not give it away to credit card companies.

- When you pay off your credit card every month, you have a higher credit rating. Not only does this make you feel good, but it also helps you save money later.

A Story

I didn't really ever think much about my credit rating. I wasn't allowed to have a credit card growing up (mostly because my mom had one when she was growing up that her parents paid, and my dad wanted me to experience a different lifestyle). It wasn't until I was in my senior year of college that I realized it would make life easier, as I could carry less cash around and have a card in case of emergencies; for example, my car breaking down or a large surprise energy bill. I had always lived within my own means, and so it was easy to use the card and then pay it off online immediately. I was much too afraid to wait until the end of the month for fear that I would have debt. To be frank, I really didn't understand credit cards, but I knew I didn't want to pay the credit card company more than I had to. I used my card for groceries and clothes shopping, and then eventually got a Macy's card so I could shop their sales. With two credit cards I felt like a pretty big deal!

It wasn't until later, after I was married and looking to buy a house, that I found out exactly how good my credit score was. It was even higher than my husband's! Because of our high credit scores we were able to get a better interest rate on our house and pay less during the largest purchase of our lives. I was also able to waive security deposits with my electricity and cable companies because of how high my credit score was. Needless to say, a high credit score can really save you money later, so it makes sense to pay it off on time every month!

> **Note:** Of course, this isn't always possible, and I completely understand that sometimes you can't pay your card(s) off every month. The point is to keep the goal of paying off your bills every month and only approach a credit card from the mind-set that you should work to pay it off quickly. If you get a credit card and think it's free money, you are in for a world of hurt later on. Make sure you can at least pay the minimum payment, and move toward fully paying the card off from there.

Have an Emergency Fund Equal to Three-to-Six Months' Living Expenses

What if the worst happens? What if you lose your job? It happens to the best of us, including me. You need to be prepared just in case, especially as a young employee who is probably easier to cut than a long-standing employee if finances get tough at your company. This emergency fund can also be helpful if your car breaks down, or if you have a huge, unexpected financial hardship (e.g., the security deposit my sister encountered when she graduated).

A Story

I was laid off from one of my first jobs when the firm downsized. I got the call literally an hour after hearing that I needed to put $1,000 into my car to pass the smog test and be able to drive. My boss called and said that as of 5 p.m. that day I wouldn't receive a paycheck, and that was that. I was living on my own with a rent that was already pretty high to begin with. Needless to say, I freaked out. The first thing I did when I got home was apply for unemployment and rework my budget to keep myself from going homeless.

If I had an emergency fund, it wouldn't have been quite as stressful! The end of the story was that I was lucky enough to get another job within two days, but that is not an adequate emergency plan! Be prepared and know that you may need to have backup options and a Plan B, C, and D for when life doesn't go the way you think it will.

Another (More Recent) Story

While writing this book, I started working for a new client. It started out great, but after a few months the relationship wasn't really working the way either of us wanted it to. I decided to put my efforts back into my own business, speaking and writing, and so we parted ways. It was a huge hit to my income, but I knew it was the right move for my career at the time. I had a good sum of money saved so my husband and I could continue to pay the mortgage and go on our planned vacation while my business continued to build. Taking the time to save money made it possible for me to do more than survive—I was able to pursue a career dream!

Try to Keep Loans to Only House Loans

Obviously this is pretty impossible for most recent graduates. This blueprint should be your guiding plan, but make it work for your life. Pay off any student loans quickly, and try to pay off your car completely. (One of the best ways to do this is to buy a less expensive car than you probably want to have!) The point to this part of your blueprint is that you don't want to be paying off anything that depreciates in value, including cars, TVs, or other electronics. Save up for those purchases and pay them in full so you don't have to pay interest on something that loses value every day. To sum up: the only reason to use credit is to buy appreciating items, not depreciating items.

Put Money Away for Long-Term Goals

Obviously, this includes retirement, but it also includes buying a house, your next car, weddings, large vacations, and other expenses. Just as we covered above, you want to save up and pay for large items up front, so you are paying off less monthly and keeping money that would be paid in interest. Now, don't worry. This does not have to be a huge sum of money going away every month. Start small and *build the habit* of pulling money out of your paycheck now. Start with $25. Pull $25 out of your paycheck every month and put it in a different account where it can earn interest. Then, as you start to make more, put more away.

> **Tip:** The hardest $10,000 to save is the first $10,000. Yet once you have the first $10,000 saved, it builds substantial interest off itself, making it easier to earn more money more quickly. Subsequent amounts are easier to save and earn.

Your Job and Finances

Ever wonder what to ask when human resources hands you a pile of forms, most of which may seem like a different language? Fret not! Thanks to Eric, I've listed many of the questions you need to ask, and what you need to worry about now that you are a full-fledged adult. The items I'll list for you are all important for you to understand, and feel free to have candid conversations with your employer about any of them. It is best for you to know upfront what you should expect, or hope to receive, from your employer. I'll be frank, I didn't know these when I first set out on my own—but I wish I had!

A quick disclaimer: There may be odd cases out there; in fact, I am one of them. But my goal in this chapter is to give you a general idea of what to expect from an employer at a typical position (where you work for one employer who pays your salary and most of your benefits costs), as well as factors you will need to consider if your employer doesn't take care of them for you.

Everything below may not apply to you, or you may have other factors in your job or financial situation that aren't listed here. If you have any financial questions or need information about something that isn't covered here, or clarification about something that is, I highly recommend that you seek out a tax advisor or financial planner. Later in this chapter I also note when you need to seek out help from a professional to help you with your finances. I can't stress enough the importance of knowing what to do with your money. The best way to do this is to find someone who you can trust to help you keep as much of it as possible! If you're not a "numbers" person, get a "numbers" person to help you. We can't know everything about everything! This chapter is meant to help you better understand your finances as a whole, and know when to seek answers to your questions (as well as what questions to ask!).

Medical Insurance

Get it. Think you can live without it? What if you accidentally fall down your stairs tomorrow and break your arm? You'll be buried in a hole of debt so early in your life that it may be hard to see the light. Many companies provide medical insurance for you. If they don't, and you are young enough, you can still get medical insurance via your parents, or you can apply for it on your own.

Here are a few things you should keep in mind:

1. Ideally you would have medical insurance through your employer so you don't have to pay anything, or only a portion of it. It is extremely common for you to have to contribute to your health insurance. This is a question to ask in your job search, or while in the process of signing on to your new job.

2. There are two main types of medical insurance: HMO and PPO.

   a. HMO: When you go to a doctor it is generally cheaper per visit, and you get to pick your primary care doctor, usually from a list of approved doctors. The doctor then gets money monthly from your insurance, whether you go to the doctor or not. They are typically the "gatekeeper." They hold the metaphoric keys that will allow you to see other specialists. You must see a primary care doctor to get a referral to see a specialist from within that group.

b. PPO: There is more flexibility, but more out-of-pocket expenses for you. If you have any special conditions, or feel that you need to see specialists often, the PPO option could be better for you, even though you might need to pay more. In a PPO situation, the PPO pays the doctor when you see them, and it can be any doctor you choose within the network. You can self refer to see a specialist, and the network of available doctors is typically larger than an HMO network.

3. There are also HSA (Health Saving Account)-compatible health plans. These are high-deductible health insurance options. Either you or your employer put money into an account on a pretax basis, and then you can use the money to pay medical expenses before being taxed on the money. This makes sense for some people, so be sure to check it out!

4. While writing this book, the Affordable Care Act passed, so I do not have a lot of detail, but please be sure to check out the marketplace for purchasing individual insurance.

A Story

I will be in so much trouble when my dad reads this . . . but the truth is that I went almost a year without health insurance. Was that stupid? Yes, completely. I didn't get medical insurance through my job, and at the time I couldn't get benefits through my parents. I attempted to get it personally, but couldn't because of past injuries. I was upset, but there wasn't anything I could do. I ate a lot of vitamins and was extremely careful trying not to break anything or get sick. I was extremely lucky to not need any medical attention that year. Medical expenses are very high, and not having health insurance is an easy way to rack up a huge amount of debt. I was eventually able to add on to my parents' health insurance until I got married, and now I have it through my husband. Get health insurance any way you can!

Questions you should ask your employer (either before you're hired, or now if you are already on the job and don't know the answers!):

1. Am I limited to a certain network of doctors to receive full medical benefits?

2. How much of the insurance is employer paid? How much do I have to pay (known as the premium)? Is my portion paid pretax or after tax?

3. How much does the employer or employee pay for dependents' medical insurance (if you have any dependents)?

4. Is there a deductible? After the deductible, is there a copay? When do I have to pay a copay?

5. How much does it cost for me to get prescription drugs?

6. What is my maximum out-of-pocket cost per year under each option?

Tip: Remember that you need to find a job that provides you with what you need. Anything your employer doesn't provide for medical insurance will have to come out of your own pocket, so use this as a negotiating point. Realize that you can ask for higher pay if they don't offer full medical benefits, or poor medical benefits. Or ask for better medical benefits if you can't ask for higher pay.

Dental Insurance

Just like medical insurance, dental insurance is important to keep you healthy and happy. Getting checked regularly at your dentist will save you from mountains of dental work later in life, ultimately saving you money!

Questions to ask your employer:

1. Is there a deductible for my dentist visits?

2. Does the deductible apply to cleanings?

3. Are there different deductibles for different services?

4. Is the insurance 100 percent employer paid?

5. Are there a lot of dentists I can go to? Are there some that are not allowed? (This is important if you have a dentist you want to go to!)

Life Insurance

This may not seem super important to you right now at twenty-something years old, but it's important to plan for the future now. And God forbid, if the worst happens to you, it helps your family after you are gone. You should definitely have life insurance if someone is financially dependent on you and would suffer financially in the event of your death. You also want to be diligent in naming beneficiaries and keeping them current; think about it this way, you don't want your life insurance to be paid to an ex and your family gets nothing.

Questions to ask your employer:

1. Is life insurance employer paid?

2. How much life insurance do I get?

3. Is there an option to pay for more life insurance? If yes, is it guaranteed issue (can I get it no matter what)? Or do I have to pass underwriting to get it?

4. Are there times throughout the year that I can change/add to my life insurance if I want?

Disability Insurance

Disability insurance is very underappreciated, but it is a big deal to you and your future. If something bad happens and you are disabled, you need disability insurance to live off while you can't work. This is really critical as a just-in-case plan, and it will save you from having to dip into all that money you've saved over the years. Typically, disability insurance is 60 percent or 66 percent of what you make at the point of disability, which means that if you are making $100 per day, you would receive $60 or $66 per day while on disability.

Questions to ask your employer:

1. Would I be covered by a disability policy?

2. Is the benefit taxable?

3. Do you provide additional benefits over state or social security?

4. Is there a waiting period? What is it? With disability insurance there can be a waiting period (thirty, sixty, ninety days) in which you won't get paid.

5. What is the percentage benefit? 60 percent or 66 percent?

6. Is there a cap on the benefit? So much per month before it shuts off?

7. What is the maximum time period it can go? Two years, five years, or by age? (Some shut off at sixty or sixty-five years old.)

8. What is the definition of disability? (This can vary widely and have a big impact on your ability to collect benefits.)

Stock Options

Now on to fun things that can make you money! Stock options are where your company gives you the right to purchase stock at the current price over a long period of time, whereas other people outside of the company may have to pay much more per share. Example: You can buy shares at the current price (regardless of what happens to be the actual price for nonemployees) for the next ten years. There are a few important key terms to remember about stock options.

Vesting Schedule

The option to purchase usually vests over a four- to five-year period of time. This means you can't actually buy or receive the stock until after those four to five years. You might have access to part of the stock after a year, another portion after another year, and so on. It takes longer for you to have access to all of it, and it is purposefully meant as an incentive for you to stay with the company longer.

Exercise Price

This is the price the company sets the stock at for you (i.e., the price you'll have to pay per share).

Expiration

Typically the stock option expires after ten years (it can be shorter or longer), so after the four to five years it vests and you have five to six years to buy it before it expires. If you quit your job, you generally only have ninety days to exercise your right to buy what is available.

Same-Day Sale

Your company allows you to "exercise" your option and keep the "profit" (the difference between the exercise price and the current price).

A Story

As a young entrepreneur, this was an important piece to my finances, and I didn't understand it. I consulted a startup for a few years, and as a bonus they gave me stock options. I was really excited, and thought it meant free money! This was not necessarily the case. Stock options can be risky, especially with a startup. The company wasn't public, so I couldn't purchase the stock or watch it, as well as the fact that there wasn't a guarantee the stock would ever go on the market. Then I would have had to work for the company for an additional four years to receive all the stock that they offered me, which I didn't end up doing. And after all of this, I would have then had to purchase the shares, which didn't seem as exciting. All this to say, you don't have to be a traditional corporate employee for stock options to be important to your finances. It is important to read any documents or contracts you are given to truly understand what you are getting and when. If possible, have a lawyer or financial planner help you understand what you are reading completely.

There are important-to-understand tax implications to purchasing stock options. There are two types of stock options: incentive stock options and nonqualified stock options. Both have tax implications, and you should consult a tax advisor as soon as you get either one.

Questions you should ask your employer:

1. What is the vesting schedule?

2. What is the exercise price?

3. What is the expiration date?

4. What is the waiting period if I leave the company?

5. Are the stock options incentive or nonqualified? (This is just for your tax advisor to know.)

6. Does the company allow 83B elections? You don't need to worry about what this means, but your tax advisor will need to know. Take as many notes as you can during this conversation so you can fully explain it to your tax advisor and learn about all your options and how you can make the most money.

7. Does the company offer "same day" sale?

Section 125 Cafeteria Plan

This is a program in which you can elect to take money out of your paycheck and put it toward medical expenses (copay, etc.) or daycare costs, and all of this money is *pretax*. This means if you have young children, you can put money away *before taxes* to go toward their childcare expenses!

Generally you can plan how much you want to put away, so make sure you plan for the year and understand what you will need to budget for each year. You might not be able to get anything back at the end of the year, so only put away money you think you will actually spend. This can include glasses, braces, retainers, or any other planned medical expenses you know you generally make.

Questions to ask your employer:

1. How much can I put away per paycheck?

2. If I don't use it all in the calendar year, is it gone?

3. Do I qualify to participate in the childcare program?

4. What medical expenses qualify under the medical reimbursement program?

Retirement

I'll be honest, this word lives in the top ten of things I'm afraid of! As a self-employed twenty-something, I'm terrified about saving up for retirement and count my blessings every day that I married an engineer with a steady paycheck and retirement plan. What I learned while researching for this chapter, however, is that it doesn't have to be as scary as I think it is. As mentioned earlier, consistency is key, and *building the habit early* is the best thing you can do to set yourself up for success.

Questions to ask your employer:

1. What type of retirement plan do you offer? Sometimes companies refer to their 401k plans as retirement plans. If so, be sure you understand how that affects your potential earning power.

2. Does your organization offer a pension program?

3. Is there a waiting period before participating in a retirement plan?

4. How much does the employer put into my plan?

5. What is the vesting schedule?

6. How much can I put into my own retirement plan? What are the monthly limits?

7. Are there matching contributions? (i.e., if you put a certain amount in, will your employer match it?)

8. What investment choices do I have? If you don't want to be involved in deciding how much stocks or bonds are in your portfolio or account, there is generally a mutual fund manager from an investment management company that can take care of it.

9. If I put an amount in, how does that affect my paycheck?

10. What happens if I leave the company? How do I keep what I've earned? (Sometimes companies will give you a set amount of time to transfer the money before you lose it.)

11. What tools or resources are available to help me make decisions? (i.e., how much to invest, put away, etc.)

Tip: Make sure that if your company offers a retirement plan or tool—and they are willing to "match" some of your contributions—use it! Matching contributions are free money, so be sure to take advantage of any that are offered to you.

Another Tip: If you are like me and don't have the traditional 9-to-5 job, you may not have a retirement plan option. If this is the case, I promise it isn't the end of the world! Be sure to put money away for retirement on your own. You can start by simply putting money into a savings account. Then you can lock larger amounts of money into a high-yield savings account, potentially even an account that you can't access as often, which will offer you higher interest percentages.

All of the questions listed earlier for any of these plans, programs, and options will set you up to successfully negotiate everything you need or want from your new employer. Not to mention, you will look as if you really know what you're talking about! You are an extremely capable professional, after all. Next I will cover a few more financial items that you should keep in mind while making the transition from student to adult.

Insurance

We've covered medical and dental, but there are many other types of insurance. A few for you to keep in mind, and hopefully get, are renter's insurance or homeowner's insurance. These are important in case someone breaks into your residence and takes anything of value, or in the event of a fire in your home.

A Story

One of my friends was engaged and had moved into a new apartment. They were getting close to the wedding and had all of their wedding gifts, wedding rings, and other items in their apartment. A few months before the wedding, their house was broken into and everything was stolen, including their wedding bands! It was horrible, and something no couple needs to deal with that close to their special day. Luckily, they had renters' insurance and were able to get reimbursed for everything taken. (I can only hope they'd already written all their thank-you notes and didn't miss anyone!)

Another insurance, which you hopefully already have, is auto insurance. It is illegal to drive without it, and with how much cars cost, you really should have it anyway. Car accidents happen often, and the smallest fender bender can cost thousands of dollars. You can also get insurance that includes roadside assistance and reimbursement for the theft of items from your car.

Tip: Do not just get the minimum amount of car insurance that your state requires. These limits are rarely enough. Consult an independent car insurance salesperson regarding recommendations about the limits you REALLY should have.

Another insurance, which I don't have but have seriously considered, is pet insurance. If you worry about the cost of your pet's vet bill or potential health problems your pet might have, pet insurance might be a great option for you. They have options for accidents, general health, and more. You pay a monthly fee and take your pet in for regular checkups to make sure your pet is staying healthy.

A Story

Betsy's beloved yellow lab, Max, racked up big medical bills during his first year of life, including major shoulder surgery. Ironically, Betsy considered pet insurance but decided against it. This, of course, is a decision she now regrets! Pets are an important part of our lives, and we want them to live happy, healthy lives. This can get expensive. Talk to your vet about plans he/she has available!

If you are rough on your electronics, you also might want to consider extended warranties. I happen to drop my phone every chance I get, and have been known to drop it out of windows on the freeway, in toilets, and under cars. Therefore, I get the top insurance available for my phones so that—no matter what I do—I get a brand new phone when mine is broken. Make sure you really understand yourself and whether it's worth it for you to purchase an insurance plan or warranty for any of your larger purchases. As our generation gets more and more mobile, it means we carry more expensive things around with us, which can lead to more dropping and, unfortunately, breaking.

Jewelry is another insurance option you might want to consider. Some jewelers even offer insurance for theft! If you have any diamonds or expensive gemstones, be sure to get a warranty or insurance plan in which you can bring the ring in regularly to check the attachment prongs to make sure you don't lose your stones unnecessarily.

Taxes

Is tax time your least favorite time of the year? It doesn't have to be! If you plan appropriately, it can actually be a happy time because you can get some money back. Here is the best recommendation for setting yourself up for success with taxes: Once you know how much you will be paid, do a calculation to see if your tax withholding is done appropriately. There are a few ways to do this, including tax software, downloading the forms from irs.gov and doing the calculations yourself, or seeing a tax person for his/her opinion.

Plan to pay in enough to generate a tax refund at the end of the year. Sometimes you even get a nice check that you can then spend on fun things, or put away to save for some of those larger purchases we talked about.

Tip: If you don't have the traditional 9-to-5 job (such as a freelancer or contractor), be sure that you are putting money away from each paycheck toward taxes. This should be in a different account from your savings, because you WILL owe taxes at the end of the year. My friend Anne and I both learned this the hard way when we started our nontraditional jobs and then owed money at the end of the year. You can go to the IRS website or consult your tax advisor to learn how much (percentage of your income) you should put away to be safe at tax time.

Be Patient

The most important thing to keep in mind with your finances is to be patient. It's human nature to want it all and want it all right now. This is evident in our culture with most people's horrible credit card debt. The problem with wanting it all right now is that it can only be sustained temporarily, and it isn't a long-term standard of living.

A great example of this is Eric's story about wanting that huge, flat-screen TV on sale. And in this scenario, even though it's on sale, you really can't afford it. You decide you "need" it for your standard of living, so you buy it anyway and put it on credit. Then you're stuck paying off a TV instead of saving the money and being able to buy more of what you want later. You really couldn't afford the TV that you didn't need in the first place. Moral of the story: be patient and don't buy things until you can afford them! There will always be another Memorial Day weekend and another Memorial Day weekend sale. I repeat—there will ALWAYS BE ANOTHER SALE, so don't feel pressured to buy something now just because it's on sale.

Do you want to be a millionaire? Most people do. Anyone reading this book can be a millionaire—just start putting money away monthly now. Automate your savings to come out of your paycheck and deposit into a separate account if possible so you don't even know it's missing. That way, there are no excuses, and it will build without you even paying attention. You can do it! We believe in you!

CHEAT SHEET

- Create your blueprint with the end in mind
  - Live below your income
  - Pay off your credit cards every month
  - Have an emergency fund equal to three-to-six months' living expenses
  - Try to keep loans to only house loans
  - Put money away for long-term goals

- Your job and finances

- Medical insurance

- Dental insurance

- Life insurance

- Disability insurance

- Stock options
  - vesting schedule
  - exercise price
  - expiration
  - same-day sale

- Cafeteria/Section 125

- Retirement

- Insurance

- Taxes

- Be patient

Source: Eric P. Martin, CFP, Martin, Wardin & Eissner Financial Group
www.mwefinancial.com

CHAPTER THREE
LIVING ALONE OR WITH OTHERS
Tori

A Story

The spring break before I graduated from college in Fresno, California, I drove back to my hometown in the San Francisco Bay Area on a mission—I was going to find an apartment and put down a deposit on it. I didn't have a job (or any job prospects), no roommate, and really no plan besides "I'll figure it out!" I knew I couldn't move back in with my parents, because—while I love them with all my heart—we simply don't get along (as well) when I'm under their roof.

I wanted my freedom, and I'd had enough horrible experiences with college roommates to know that living with someone else probably wasn't for me either. I liked my space and wanted to keep it that way. So I found the perfect loft apartment, put down the deposit, and said my prayers. A month later, I had my full-time job for postgraduation. I moved out of my college apartment the day of graduation and moved into my Bay Area apartment the next day.

Now, you may not be like me, and roommates may be your way to go. I just wanted to give you a glimpse into the decision I made and why. Young adults fresh out of college have a lot of decisions to make, and the decision whether to move home, move out on your own, or move in with roommates is a complicated, personal one. It will affect how you live day to day, especially if you plan on telecommuting or working from home, and it will affect your relationships with anyone you choose to live with.

So which decision is the right one for you? Let's break down some of the pros and cons of living on your own versus living with others.

Living at Home

When you graduate, even if you have a job and especially if you're moving back from a college area to your hometown, sometimes the easiest thing to do is to move home for a while so you can figure out where you want to live, save up for a security deposit and rent, or even save money to buy a condo, townhouse, or home.

I've known several people who have chosen this route, and it's worked for them. I'm going to share with you what these friends felt were the upsides of their living situations, as well as a few tips to get the most out of living at home with the least amount of drama.

Cost-Effectiveness

This one is pretty obvious, but it may not always be the case. Some parents do want you to pay rent, so then you need to negotiate a price that makes the most sense for all of you. If you plan on moving out soon, maybe make an agreement that the rent start really low, and then slowly starts to increase if you don't move out. This will make them happy knowing there's an end date and put a fire under you to find that great place you want.

Home-Cooked Meals

My friends who had moved home were all made dinners and had food around the house at all times. I would be lying if I said I wasn't jealous.

A Story

While I decided to move out on my own, as I mentioned above, I also decided to move back to my hometown, about two exits and five minutes away from my parents' house. While this afforded me a lot of freedom, I quickly learned that if I didn't buy food, it didn't show up in my fridge. I had a love-hate relationship with grocery shopping, and so I generally had little to no food. Living that close to my parents gave me some perks, including going to their house for dinner if I was short on cash or if my fridge was empty except for moldy cheese and old jam. My parents were great about helping me out, because they knew I was on my own for the first time and I was bound to make some mistakes. Not buying food was an easy one to remedy.

Convenience

Moving back home is convenient. You probably still have stuff there, you know the place, your parents are there to watch the house when you go away, and it's probably comfortable and safe. It's a lot less scary than jumping into a brand new situation either by yourself or with people you don't know.

Security

Living with others is safer than living on your own. There's someone at the house to come home to; it's not an empty, dark house. You also have others in the house for when you hear that loud noise you swear is a person but is really a tree branch.

Support

Need help making huge life decisions? How to deal with a friend who isn't being friendly, or what outfit to wear? Living with your parents can be a great resource for all the decision process help you'll need. This can also extend to financial support in some cases; if you're running low on cash you might be able to pick up a few extra chores or they can work out a situation in which you can pay them back.

For some of you these reasons for living at home will outweigh any reasons not to. If you are one of those, I applaud you. I've seen many of these situations work out well, and many of my friends came to respect their parents even more after living with them. The trick is that you also have to want to make it work.

How to Live at Home Successfully

Based on many conversations that I've had, including researching for this book and interviews with people that I know, there are many ways you can go above and beyond to make living at home a harmonious experience.

Be Respectful

This is above and beyond the most important step. It is your parents' house and, especially if you aren't paying to live there, you need to respect both their space and them as your landlords. Take care of their things, replace things you break, clean up after yourself, and show them that you appreciate their hospitality. Doing anything less will cause arguments and potentially strain your relationship, and it may lead to them not wanting you to live there anymore.

Confront the Little Things

Let your parents know when things are bothering you. It's much better to establish potential boundaries when things are small than wait until it's too late.

A Story

One of my friends lived at home, and her mom would text her every day to see when she would be home for dinner. It was nice at first, but after a while, she realized it was a habit that was forming, in which her mom wanted to know when she would be home every night and she felt as if she wasn't being as independent as she could or wanted to be. As soon as it started bothering her, she brought it up to her mom and told her that while she really appreciated her mom making her food, she needed to be able to come and go as she needed. After their conversation, her mom would just plan on her not being there and package any leftovers for her to eat later. It worked out well for them, and, because it was handled early on, there wasn't any tension or argument.

Go Above and Beyond

This doesn't mean you have to do everything for them every time the opportunity arises, but it does mean doing a thing or two here or there.

Walk the dog for them if they might be home late, even if they don't ask you to. Empty the dishwasher if it's clean, and you know they will appreciate it later. Doing these small things once in a while, without expecting anything back, will put a very positive spin on you living at home.

Act Like an Adult

Your parents are adults. Treat them that way and they'll treat you better in return. Let them know what is OK and not OK with your new living arrangement, but instead of screaming, pouting, or holding your breath, take a grown-up angle and tackle problems with a thought-out argument and discussion. Your parents still think you're the eighteen-year-old, know-it-all kid who left their house to go to college. Prove to them you are now a twenty-something, educated, mature adult.

Have Fun and Learn

Use this opportunity as a positive experience to finally learn old secret family recipes, or have your dad show you how to fix something on your car or in the house. You (hopefully) will never have this experience again, so get the most out of it and enjoy it.

If you do everything above, you're much more likely to be happy at home and hopefully save a few bucks to move out on your own someday, or to hold out for the job you've always wanted. If, however, you just can't seem to make living at home work, you have two other options: living with roommates or living on your own.

Living with a Roommate(s)

Similar to living at home, living with a roommate means you have to learn to live well with others. You'll notice a few of the reasons for living with a roommate are similar to the ones for living at home, but there is a big difference between living with your parents versus living with friends. We'll cover how to find the best roommate, how to be a good roommate, and what to do if you've tried everything but it just isn't working out.

Reasons to Live with a Roommate

Cost-Effective

This is the single most common reason most people move in with a roommate or two or three. Every bill is at least cut in half. You'll save a lot of money this way between rent, electricity, Internet, cable, and more. You can also split groceries, and cooking for two or three (or more) usually saves you money versus cooking for one. (And you'll have to cook less often, which is certainly a bonus!)

Also, when you live with others you can usually afford to live in a bigger place. With two or more people footing the bill, you can afford that extra square footage and balcony, or maybe something the same size but in a better neighborhood. These are all things to consider when you're looking around, as living on your own can get very expensive very quickly.

Companionship

Even if you don't move in with your best friend, or aren't close to the person you move in with, there will be someone to talk to, and it will be more difficult to get lonely. You won't come home to an empty apartment or house every night, and you'll have someone to share your new experiences with. You'll have more chances to go out, find new places to go (everyone has their regular spots), and things like recreational activities are more fun with more people.

A Story from Betsy

When I graduated from college, I moved in with my best friend, and we had a ton of fun for the first year after we both graduated. Then, she decided to go to graduate school in another city, so I was left without someone to live with. I really didn't want to live alone, so I asked an acquaintance to move in with me as she and I had hit it off and I thought she would be a good roommate. Well, she was a good roommate, but she got laid off from her job right after she moved in. The thought of finding a new roommate was not appealing to me, and I loved my apartment and having companionship, so I paid her half of the rent for two months after she got laid off and was looking for another job. That was worth it to me.

Convenience

Having a roommate means having a live-in house sitter. If you need to go on a trip, they can water your plants, take care of the apartment or house, gather the mail, and even feed a pet if you have one.

Security

When you aren't at home, there is someone else there to make sure things are safe. Plus, if you live in a less-than-desirable neighborhood, there is someone in the house to come back to and who expects you in case you don't come back on time.

A Story

When I lived on my own I had one very scary experience. I came home late one night and someone had scratched obscenities and that they wanted me to die on the door. While I'm pretty sure no one I knew would do that (specifically because they spelled the word *die* wrong—*dye*), I wasn't willing to discuss that with whomever I might find standing at my door with a weapon. I called the police and stayed at my parents' house for a week while I discussed safety measures with my complex (which was locked down, and very odd that the person was even able to get in) and they replaced the door. Needless to say, it shook me up, but nothing ever came from it. Living with someone else means the small stuff will be easier to let go, and you can feel camaraderie in the spookier times.

Support

Does this purse match this dress? What should I get mom or dad for their birthday? These questions can be thrown back and forth between roommates, and a roommate can be an excellent idea if you like to bounce ideas around. Your roommate could even be someone to get advice from on your love life, or work life, or other important decisions.

Chores

You can split the chores! It's a lot less work on you when you only have to vacuum every other time, or you can take turns grocery shopping.

Or you can negotiate different chores, so you take out the trash but your roommate washes the dishes. This is especially great if you hate washing the dishes (like I do) but don't mind cleaning floors. It lightens the load for both of you and gives you more free time.

Diversity

Everyone is different, and living with a roommate is a fantastic opportunity to learn important lessons about different cultures, people, and beliefs. You will also learn a lot about yourself. Developing social skills and knowing how you deal with particular situations (and how other people may react differently) is a vital part of growing up. Having a roommate will also help train you to better deal with different, or difficult, types of people—especially when you think about the fact that you may need to work with someone like them later on.

Reasons Not to Live with a Roommate

Here are a few reasons we'd advise you to consider carefully when deciding whether or not to move in with a roommate. These are probably not the best reasons to move in with a roommate, but these are why many people choose to live with another person.

Logic

You move in with someone who is in a similar situation because it just "makes sense." While it may make sense to others, it still may not be the right decision. That person may have completely different ideas about what being a roommate really is, or may have very different habits than you. Just because you are in the same city doesn't mean you will get along well. Remember to be subjective and choose what makes the most sense for your life.

Habit

You've always had a roommate, and so when you graduate and move on you automatically look for another one. Pause for a moment and think about the reasons above and below (in the living alone section) to see if living with a roommate is really something you want. Just because it worked with the person you lived with before doesn't mean it will work again with a new person.

Peer Pressure

Everyone else lives with a roommate, so you should as well. Or you're worried you might come across as a loner because no one wants to live with you. Keep in mind that this is your decision. It shouldn't matter what others are doing around you, or what they think about your situation. Believe me, when you list the reasons you choose to live alone versus with roommates, they might be a little jealous! If the pressure comes from your finances, adjust your monthly budget to see if you can make it work. Decide whether living on your own is more important than shoes, video games, or eating out as often.

Find the Right Roommate

So you've decided to move in with a roommate, and you may have a few friends in mind or someone that you think could potentially be a good fit. Put in the extra effort to make sure that this is a person you can live with every day, and you'll be more likely to have a great experience. Here are a few tips to help you make sure you've found "the one" (or two, or three).

Rental History

What is their rental history? This will help you know if they tend to bounce around a lot, or if they are in it for the long haul. Have they had roommates before? If so, how did they get along with them? (Verify this if possible, especially if the potential roommate is a friend-of-a-friend who used to live together.) Why did they leave their apartments/living situations? This will give you good insight into how they handle their problems and whether you can expect them to move out if you have a disagreement.

Financial Feasibility

Do they have enough money to cover the bills? This includes rent, electricity and gas, Internet, cable (if you want it), potentially water and garbage fees, renter's insurance, and anything else you think might come up. Do they have enough to split the security deposit? You don't want to be left with these fees hanging over your head and coming out of your wallet. If you're moving in with more than one person, you can always adjust these bills based on who uses what, which rooms are bigger, and other factors. Put it all in writing so you have the same understanding of what bills to expect. Let's repeat that. PUT IT ALL IN WRITING, and have each roommate sign a "roommate agreement." Trust us, this makes life so much easier! (We'll talk more about roommate agreements later on in this chapter.)

Sleep Schedule

Are they an early riser or night owl? You may think the times that you personally go to bed and wake up are the best times for everyone, but that is hardly ever the case, and it isn't something you can change about the other person. If you need to be up at 5:30 a.m. every day to get to work and want to go to bed early, make sure you find someone who can respect that, or better yet, has similar habits.

A Story

While my husband, David, loved living with his roommate after college, there were many times when his roommate was unemployed (or on a different schedule than David was) and would go to bed hours after he did. Those hours when David was trying to sleep and his roommate was awake, he'd be playing video games with a headset in, having loud, heated "discussions" with other players. David asked him to keep it down and be quiet (as their walls were paper thin), but even when he wasn't chatting with other players at two in the morning, the surprises he'd encounter in the game would often still cause him to shout out obscenities or yell out. David knew it wasn't purposeful or malicious, but even with earplugs it would be loud enough to keep David up for hours. The relationship and roommate situation was worth it for David, but it is definitely something you want to think about when moving in with someone new.

Temperature Comfort Levels

What temperature do they think is comfortable? What are their feelings toward using the air conditioner or heater? You may love to be cold, but they might prefer to be hot (or at least warm). This is important to discuss as it will affect your body daily and your wallet monthly.

A Story

I grew up without air conditioning. We lived in the San Francisco Bay Area and rarely needed it. When I moved into an apartment with someone else, I was used to not having it and never wanted to turn it on, because I didn't want to pay for it. My roommates always wanted to use it and, because we were very immature, it became a passive aggressive battle of turning it off and on. This could have been easily solved if we'd talked about it, but we didn't and had completely different understandings of comfortable temperatures.

Entertainment

How much TV do they watch? How often are they on their computer/using the Internet? This is a good indicator of how much they will be around the apartment, and it also includes part of question #1: whether you should pay for these items, and if so, whether you should split them in half. It also might be a good indicator that you should get your own TV, or have a multiple TV household. If you both like to watch TV but not the same shows, it would save you a lot of arguments later on.

A Story

David and his best friend were roommates for years, and they both knew that they liked to watch their own shows and play video games, but neither wanted to have to leave the living room. Their solution? Have two huge TVs in the living room so they could both watch/play next to each other. It looked a little odd (they were placed right next to each other on two totally different styles of entertainment centers), and it was definitely a bachelor's solution, but it is a great idea for those who don't want to give up the space or compromise on what to watch. David could watch baseball games while his roommate played games and watched Netflix. It was a win-win. A unique win-win, but a win-win nonetheless!

Noise Levels

What level of noise are they used to? Do they like to have the TV on, or music blaring while they are at home? Do they prefer quiet reading or napping? If you are the music blaster, remember that you need to be respectful to them as well. If your roommate wants to read a book every day when they get home and you like to blast your music, it will cause arguments, and you won't have an optimal living situation.

Religious Views

What are their religious views? Are they liberal or conservative? You know, you're never supposed to talk about sex, religion, or politics at the dinner table, but when you're living with someone it's bound to come up. If either of you have dead-set views one way or the other, it might be better to look other places. If you feel you can listen or discuss in a friendly, banterlike manner, then it may be an OK decision for you. This is completely subjective and your choice, but just be aware that it could potentially cause issues.

A Story

My dad is a very conservative Christian man, but his best friend is very liberal. My husband is also a conservative Christian, and his best friend is a liberal Atheist. Both sets of friends have spent enormous amounts of time together, and my husband and his friend were roommates for years. Needless to say, different beliefs can get along and live together, you just have to find other things you both enjoy and agree upon.

Lifestyle

When should you worry about your roommate? Are they someone who comes home every night? Should you be worried if they aren't home in the morning, or if they are fifteen minutes late the night before? You may not think this will be an issue, but if they don't come home for days on end, you may not know whether to send the search party unless they tell you. Have an understanding with each other, and maybe send a courtesy text if you will be really late or not coming home.

A Story

My friend, Kim, bought a house and then took in two roommates. She had very few rules, including not lying to her and texting her if they weren't coming home at night, because she tended to worry and these girls were her friends. She didn't want to lose sleep over them not being home if they were just out late. It seemed to work out fine until one of the roommates, who happened to be dating Kim's cousin, cheated on the cousin and started staying out late multiple times with no explanation and lying to Kim about it. Kim finally confronted her to let her know that she still had a place to stay, but she had to shape up in order to continue living with her. The roommate took the hint and was much better to her after that conversation.

Chore Preferences

What chores do they prefer? As mentioned above in the reasons to live with a roommate, you can split chores! Find out if they prefer some you dislike, or if you prefer some they dislike. See if you can split them that way, and switch back and forth on the chores you both dislike.

A Story

When I got married, I had to finally look at making a roommate situation work really well, something I didn't have much luck with when I was in college and assigned to roommates. My husband and I sat down and discussed what chores we hated and which ones we could live with. We decided that whoever cooked, the other person had to clean dishes, and that I would handle laundry and grocery shopping. He would take out the trash and clean up after the pets. It was pretty easy to figure out once we sat down and decided what we were willing to do versus what we don't like to do.

Personality

Are they an extrovert or introvert? Do they want to tell you all about their problems? Or will they be quiet when they are upset and want you to leave them alone? After all, as previously mentioned, one of the perks of living with someone is having someone to talk to after a long, hard day, and that door swings both ways! Sometimes you'll have to be the sympathetic ear or the shoulder to cry on. Just make sure that you somewhat understand what your roommate needs—or is expecting. It's important to know how to best deal with your potential roommate when they are upset to keep you from overstepping your boundaries and help you achieve an optimal living situation.

Fragrance/Odor Sensitivity

Are they sensitive to fragrances/odors? This can be to perfume or cologne, cleaning supplies, room sprays, or even gym clothes. Make sure you know if there are certain smells they can't stand and try to stay away from those. If you love your smell and want to stick with it, find a different roommate who can live with it.

A Story

I moved in with one of my best friends when I was in college. We had always been really close and thought it would be the perfect living situation. She loves the smell of cinnamon; she chews cinnamon gum, lights cinnamon candles, and even has a cinnamon air freshener in her car. While the smell didn't bother me at all, my boyfriend at the time couldn't stand it. Apparently, I always smelled like cinnamon, and he refused to go into our apartment because of the smell. It became an argument between the two of them, with me in the middle, and no one won. Something as simple as smell caused serious, unneeded stress on my relationships. I'm still friends with my old roommate and that boyfriend is long gone, and, as you might expect, her house continues to always smell like delicious apples and cinnamon!

Allergies

Are they allergic to anything? This is especially important for severe allergies, or if you plan to cook for each other. Potential dangerous allergies can include peanuts, perfume, milk, seafood, flour, mold, or smoke. This can also be a deal breaker if you have a pet you want to keep and your potential roommate is allergic to it.

Cleanliness

How clean do they like to keep their space? How often do they take the trash out? Can dishes sit in the sink "soaking" overnight? Do they like to vacuum every week (or every day)? How clean do they like mirrors or windows? Are they coaster people? Think about what is important to you in your space, and make sure you can come to an agreement or compromise.

Smoking, Drinking, and Drugs

Do they smoke or do recreational drugs? If one of you is a smoker, make sure you find someone willing to live with that, or at least set ground rules (i.e., smoking outside only, or a certain distance from the apartment/house). Sometimes landlords set these rules for you—are these rules you want to enforce, or are you willing to turn a blind eye? If you can't live with the fact that someone might do something illegal in your space, you need to have that conversation now.

What about alcohol? Do they drink? How much? How often? This, too, should be discussed.

A Story

One of my husband's old roommates was, for all intents and purposes, a hippy. He rarely showered, walked around the apartment in his underwear, and was growing mushrooms in his bedroom closet for a horticultural class—a fact that he hid from his roommates. One day this roommate had a school group over to their apartment and the roommate bragged that he was actually growing shrooms (an illegal drug). One of those classmates contacted David and his other roommates and was upset about how dangerous that would be, and what it meant for them if he was caught. One of David's other roommates was extremely upset and, along with the classmate, called the police. A few days later, when David was out with some friends, he got a call from his hippy roommate who asked David if he had called the police on him. When David said he hadn't, the roommate said, "Well, someone did," as he was in handcuffs and being arrested. The police searched the apartment, but all they found were the mushrooms for his class. Needless to say, this was a huge issue that could have been resolved had the hippy roommate not lied or thought it was OK to tell others there were drugs in the apartment.

Décor Styles

What is their décor style? Are they minimalists (e.g., a folding chair and bed is fine—just the basics), or do they like to hang things every-where? What decorating style do they have? Do they like to decorate for holidays? What you think looks good might not match their opinions, and vice versa.

All of these questions should set a good foundation for knowing if this is a person you could potentially live with. While asking these questions, you may find odd (or wonderful) personality quirks. Be sure to ask them questions that will lead them to opening up. Think about it like a job interview. You want to make sure they are a good fit for your life and that you will both be happy with the situation. If only one of you is happy, it is probably not going to work.

Roommate Agreements

Another great way to ensure that you will both be happy is to draft a roommate agreement. Putting everything in writing (even if it seems silly to do so) forces you to say out loud everything you are thinking and sign to it. You may think you've agreed on everything, but there can always be misunderstandings, and a written agreement is the best way to ensure that you are both on the same page (both literally and figuratively). Also, please remember that moving in with someone is first and foremost a business decision. It affects you financially and could potentially put you into financial hardship if it doesn't work out.

Roommate agreements can be as thorough or as short as you think is necessary, depending on your situation. If you watch the TV show *Big Bang Theory*, you might be reminded of Sheldon and Leonard's roommate agreement, with clauses that include what they will do in the case of an apocalypse or if they invent time travel. Yours can be much simpler, but here are a few items that should be included in every roommate agreement.

Financial Responsibility

Write out the shares of rent and any other utilities. Write out specific amounts, if possible, or percentages to reduce confusion.

Living Arrangements

Specify who will live in which room and which spaces are common areas. You may also want to define what a common area means—where guests are allowed, where guests can and cannot sleep, and more. Bathroom usage sometimes falls into this category, as depending on where you live, you may have multiple bathrooms with one person using the bathroom that is also the "common use" bathroom (i.e., the one used by guests). The person "owning" this bathroom may feel the need to be compensated for the increased use of it—maybe once a month you help buy toilet paper, or every other month (or after a big party) you help clean it. These factors obviously will be affected by how many guests you have over, and you may feel the need to revisit these things after a while. In any case, just make sure you're on the same page. You don't want to throw a big party and have your roommate lock his bathroom door because he doesn't want guests using it!

Overnight Guests

Many apartment complexes will have rules about this for you, but make sure you come to an agreement as well. How long can they stay? How many can come at once? Is there a different rule for weekends and holidays versus weekdays? Should they give notice ahead of time (twenty-four hours, a week), and will there be a rule about coeds staying? The only difference between a roommate's significant other staying over constantly and having another roommate is that a roommate pays their share!

A Story

My sister lived in a small, four-bedroom apartment with three other people and not a lot of common space. One of her roommates decided to have her whole family over for Thanksgiving dinner at their apartment—without asking anyone. It was obviously an inconvenience on the other roommates, but they let it go. It wasn't until the roommate's mom decided she was going to move into her room and stay for months on end that my sister and her other roommates had to let management know and get her evicted. We'll discuss how best to handle these situations later, but if you come to an agreement regarding what is and is not OK early, these types of things can be avoided.

Another Story

My sister-in-law, Taylor, moved in with a really good friend who was in a serious relationship. The boyfriend ended up staying at their apartment nonstop and was always around. For Taylor it was an inconvenience because she had to make sure she was properly dressed every time she wanted to go to the bathroom. Plus, it wasn't what she signed up for. She wanted one roommate in that space, not two. And if there was another person living there, he really should pay rent, too, right?

Cleaning

Have a written understanding of who will do what chores how often and how clean you expect the common areas to be kept (e.g., bags and personal items on the floor or table tops). Under most roommate agreements, your room is your own space, but you can write in something about smells if you find it appropriate.

A Story

My sister-in-law, from the story above, had another experience with a different roommate, where her room smelled awful. She couldn't figure out what the smell was until one day when they opened the door and the roommate was growing mushrooms in her room. This was not OK with Taylor and her other roommates, for obvious reasons including the smell, and they had to deal with it after the fact.

Purchases

If this is your, or your roommate's, first time living out in the big world, chances are you don't have a lot of belongings to fill your new space. Maybe you're both OK with this, or maybe you both decide you want a coffee table. In any case, it's important to discuss how such expenses will be paid. Will you split the cost of the table? Or are there two items and you each pay for one? Shopping together on these things is key; it's not only a good bonding experience, but you can be sure you both get something you like. Just make sure that you have a clear agreement as to who actually owns what. They may be communal items now, but when you part ways divvying up furniture can be an added stress to the moving process.

Be a Good Roommate

After you've found the person you want to live with and signed your roommate agreement, the best thing you can do (for your *own* happiness) is to be a good roommate. You want to focus on being positive and bringing the best you can, as this encourages reciprocation.

I encourage you to adopt the following rule when living with roommates (or new people in general), and I'll discuss it in detail. My husband and I learned this rule while we were in marriage counseling, and it has saved us from countless arguments and misunderstandings.

Everyone has a different "normal." That's it. Seems simple, right? But it really is something that takes time to understand and covers every aspect of your life, especially when you live with someone else. This means that whenever it comes to doing something differently, you have to realize that neither of you are right or wrong, you were just brought up with different "normals."

An example could be something as simple as toilet paper. Some people like to have the toilet paper roll over, some people prefer under. Neither way is right or wrong, but people are just used to their "normals." A much more pressing example could be how you feel about certain holidays, or how clean you each think things should be kept.

After you understand that rule, it gets easier. Here are some other specific rules to help you live well with others.

Be Upfront about Expectations

Be upfront about what you expect from those you live with. Set boundaries early and stick with them. If you let someone get away with something for a long time, even though it drives you crazy, and then blow up at them when they continue to do it, the situation probably won't end well.

Try to Say "Yes" Often

Try to say "yes" as often as possible, and realize that you might not be the easiest person to live with at all times, either. The more you can say yes to your roommate, the more often they will be willing to reciprocate, and the happier you'll both be.

Respect Your Roommate

Respect the other person, and their space. We mentioned this earlier, and we're saying it again because it is very important and encompasses a lot of the other rules. Always ask before borrowing things, or eating things, and have a clear understanding of who owns what so you know what's yours to take care of or leave alone.

Stick to Your Word and Follow Through

Stick to your word and follow through with what you tell your roommate you will do. Whether it's cleaning, calling your landlord about a repair, or paying them back for something, do it.

Compromise

This is a huge one, and will be important any time you live with anyone. If you aren't willing to take a step toward compromise and happiness, the other person won't be either. Take the first step and it will be easier for the other person.

Clean Up After Yourself

This falls under respecting your roommate and your living space, but you want to make sure that you do your part of the cleaning. This includes having good hygiene and making sure your room is somewhat tidy. It will show that you care about the space where you live.

Be Aware of Your Roommate's Sleeping Habits

Be aware of your roommate's sleeping habits, and try to respect them. Don't let your alarm clock ring for minutes on end if they are trying to sleep, and don't stumble in yelling into your phone late at night if they need to get up early. Also, if you go on vacation, make sure to shut your alarm clock off. That, in my opinion, is a total roommate faux pas.

Spend Quality Time with Your Roommate

Have conversations with them every day, even if they are short. Say hello and goodbye, ask them how they are doing, and show that you care. It will be easier to have difficult discussions if you have had lots of cordial ones. Plus, getting to know them should be fun and lead to better relationships and things to do. Try to have one time a week that you do something together, and try to do something nice for them every once in a while. Who knows, they might reciprocate!

Lock the Doors and Windows When You Leave

You don't want someone to break in and steal your, or your roommates, things and have it be your fault. Make sure your roommate(s) understand this rule as well so you can be sure to keep your home safe.

Be Flexible with Your Roommate's Life

If they have a huge meeting or work-related project coming up, respect their need for privacy and quiet. If they have a family emergency, see if there is anything you can do to help make their time easier. Remember the golden rule: Do unto others as you want them to do to you. This is the best step to take to make sure they reciprocate when you are in similar situations.

Communicate Early and Often

Communicate early and often with your roommate to make sure problems don't arise. If they do something that drives you crazy, don't stew on it. Bring it up. They may not even realize they are doing anything to bother you, and the situation will be over that quickly.

Control the Amount of Noise You Make

Can you listen to your music in your headphones rather than blasting it through speakers? Can you go outside to talk on the phone? Respect your roommates' space by trying to keep the noise level low.

Invite Your Roommate Out with You

Invite your roommate to come out with you, when appropriate. It will make them feel good that you want to spend time with them and help build your relationship.

Don't Make Your Rules Too Rigid

Remember that life is short, and try not to sweat the small stuff. My mom always says to pick "the hills you want to die on" and let the other stuff go. In other words, don't make everything into a big deal in your head or a big argument with your roommate, but instead try to pick what really is important to you and what you can let go and move on from.

If you follow these rules, we promise you will be on track toward an optimal living situation with your roommate(s). But sometimes, as you may already be aware, no matter what you do it just doesn't work out.

What to Do if It Doesn't Work Out

I've heard a lot of stories about what people do when they are just sick of a roommate, from calling the cops to hiding the alarm clock and greasing the doorknob so they can't get to the bathroom. As tempting as those options may be (and I admit, I laughed), those aren't the best ways to end the relationship and move forward. Remember when we said having a roommate is a business decision? That is true now more than ever. Try not to burn the bridge, realize you still have a security deposit invested, and try to find the easiest way out with the least amount of hurt feelings. Here are some things to try before simply asking them to move out.

I'll preface all of these statements with the fact that you should always be upfront with your roommate. Let them know you're not happy, but if they aren't getting the message you may need to be a little more aggressive with your actions to back up your words.

If your roommate is eating your food nonstop, start eating out. Especially if one of your issues is that they eat your food. Stop buying it. Keep certain things you want in your room (maybe even invest in a small mini fridge) and then go elsewhere to eat. If they lose the ability to have free food, moving out might seem attractive to them.

A Story

My friend, Carson, had a roommate who never paid for food but always ate whatever was in the fridge. They had a rule that they would take turns buying the groceries since they all like similar food, but this one roommate never paid his share. He would always have an excuse as to why he couldn't pay for food, but they watched him buy a lot of other things. It finally got to a breaking point, and while they were all best friends, they couldn't live with him anymore because he wanted them to pay his bills and buy him food. These types of roommates can be toxic, and they exist. Try not to let the pattern start.

If you are paying for all of the Internet and/or cable because they aren't paying their share, have the service suspended for a month or so, or change the password to your wireless router. Most cable companies will let you put a parental lock on channels as well. Explain to your roommate that you had to make some cuts because they weren't able to pay their part of the bills, or that their free ride is over and if they want the passwords, they'll have to pay what they owe. When there's no free entertainment, they might start looking elsewhere.

If you are continuously cleaning up after your roommate, stop. Chances are that when the dishes and piles of garbage start growing, they may try to find somewhere better kept. Stop laundering the towels, and only wash what you use. They might get the idea.

It's important to evaluate if these are short-term or long-term problems. Are they going through a job search, and if so, do you think they are motivated enough to get the job and pay you back? Or do they work and simply don't budget? Are they going through a rough time at their job and haven't had time to help with cleaning? Do you see the possibility that the work stress could cease? These are all things to consider and talk to your roommate about before making the decision to move out or asking them to move out.

If you feel as if you've tried everything and your roommate is simply a deadbeat that you should never have moved in with and trusted, then you have two options. You can either move out or ask them to move out. You leaving is often an easier option, but we want to provide some help in case you love your space or don't have other options and you want to get your roommate out.

First, and most importantly, make sure they are not on the lease. This doesn't mean to have them live with you illegally, but make sure you are the main leaseholder. If they are on the lease, there will have to be a lot more negotiating, and it's extremely difficult to get them off the lease because they are legally allowed to live on the premises. If they are on the lease, prepare any paperwork you will need to assume full responsibility of the lease, as well as make sure the utilities can all be put in your name. Preparing yourself before your roommate decides to move out will strengthen your position to get them moving out considerably. Talk to your landlord, and if you are the sole person on the lease, you will be able to evict your roommate. If not, you will have to follow their policies. Your landlord will know the rules.

Then it's time to talk to your roommate. There are some tips we'll share here, but keep in mind that chances are, if you really dislike living with your roommate, they probably don't like it much either. Be delicate; there's no reason to hurt their feelings or make them feel bad once you've made your decision. Think about it as a breakup, and treat your roommate with respect.

Be Prepared with a Plan

Be prepared and have a plan to present your roommate. Include who will leave and when, who will handle finding someone else to take on the lease, how you'll split shared belongings, and other issues (hopefully you took our advice above about splitting purchases and this last one is easy!). If you come with a plan, they may not agree with it, but at least you've thought it out and have arguments to support your points.

Set Up a Time to Talk

Set up a time and let the roommate know you need to talk about your living arrangement. Give them plenty of notice so they can make it. Giving them notice ahead of time also gives them time to think about it. They will most likely be less defensive rather than you telling them out of the blue. If you have multiple roommates, make sure everyone can be there.

Break Up in Person

Break up in person, and out of the house or apartment. People are less likely to get upset in public places, which you can use to your advantage. Person-to-person shows the most respect, and if you approach the situation like an adult, chances are they will, too. If you are really worried about them blowing up, perhaps consider a phone call. Or sometimes writing a letter is acceptable as well.

Keep the Discussion Short

This isn't time to dwell on every little thing that they've done to bother you. Approach this situation with a "we're moving forward" attitude, and you will be more likely to get through it quickly.

Be Straightforward

Be straightforward with your roommate. If you've done everything you can to get across the idea that they need to move out and nothing has worked, just be honest and stick with your word.

Be as Honest as You Can

Be as honest as you can, but try to keep their feelings in check. Try to avoid an argument, and keep from burning bridges, especially if your roommate is a friend or someone you will need to interact with again later.

Give Notice to Your Roommate

Give them a comfortable time period (generally fifteen to thirty days) to make sure they have time to find a new place to live and you have time to find a new roommate.

Be Prepared for Their Reaction

Be prepared for how your roommate will react. Even if you've been upfront, they still may not see this coming and there could be tears or anger. Let those feelings come out, and expect them as part of the breakup process. Don't retaliate by yelling back or crying, too. Let them react, and keep yourself together. Also, don't let their reaction force you to change your decision. Be firm in what you say and move forward.

If your roommate still wants to stay and won't leave after your discussion, then it's time to explore your legal options. Inform your roommate that you will have to get the landlord involved, and legal eviction is a messy process that will stay on their record and could prevent them from finding another place to live.

Then talk to your landlord and learn the specific rules and regulations regarding your house or apartment. Different cities and states have different rules. If at any point you feel like you are in danger because of your roommate, call the police and/or vacate the premises. Keep records of what happens so you can let the police know the background and steps that led you to needing to vacate. No property is worth you getting injured over.

A Story

This is really the end to an earlier story. When my sister-in-law, Taylor, was living with a girl who had her boyfriend over every day, it started to take a toll on Taylor. Taylor also had a cat, who the roommate and boyfriend would torment at times, and they had no respect for the common areas, burning the carpet and flooding the kitchen. But the real problem began when the boyfriend started becoming abusive to her roommate. Taylor wasn't sure what to do, but she knew she couldn't stay in a space where she was worried for her or her friend's life. After many conversations with her friend on the issue and Taylor's concerns for their safety, she decided to move out and moved in with another friend rather than trying to get the friend and boyfriend to move out. It was extremely difficult to get any part of the security deposit back, and she lost a friendship over the move.

In Taylor's case, she left the lease early. This is another option you can discuss with your landlord. She was able to talk her landlord out of additional fees, but you may have to pay them. If you only have a few months left, it may be worth the few half-rents to get out of the situation, and then you can consider taking the roommate to small claims court or consider the money lost as part of a painful lesson.

If this all sounds a little overwhelming, we get it. And totally agree. Most roommate situations rarely get that bad, but we want you to be prepared in case you are one of those rare situations.

Living Alone

When I was moving out on my own, I had been through some pretty rough roommate experiences, and knew I wanted to be on my own for a while. Even thinking about going through finding another roommate, or trying to divvy up space, make agreements, or going out of my way to make someone else happy in my own apartment was all too much for me. I was ready to take on all the responsibilities of running my own apartment, as long as it was all my space.

There are a few outstanding reasons to live on your own. This list isn't as extensive as the lists for living at home or with roommates, but for some people [me] it is enough.

Privacy

Some people like their privacy, and living alone affords you that luxury. You can walk around the place in whatever you are comfortable in and not worry about your roommate(s), or any friends they may have over, busting out of their room on you. You can watch those guilty pleasure movies without judgment, and eat ice cream whenever you feel like it. There's no one to judge you when you feel like being left alone.

Freedom

You can do whatever you want, whenever you want, with no one to answer to. You can have your friends over, stay up as late and be as loud (barring any neighborhood or complex rules) as you want, leave a mess until you want to clean it up, and put things wherever you want to put them.

A Story

I grew up with an interior designer for a mom. It was fun at times, because I had a really cool room and she would paint pretty much as often as we wanted to change our wall colors. The other side of that coin was that she staged everything and every piece had to be clean and in its place. I remember that she considered my room to be "a mess" if I had an outfit (or two or three) on the floor, or if a few staged items were out of place. When I finally moved out on my own, my favorite thing to do when I got home was to throw everything in my hands on the floor. Then I would sit on the couch and smile because there was no one to tell me differently.

Peace

As discussed earlier, having a roommate can be great, but there's also a risk of it not working out. You can get in arguments about anything from being too loud to eating each other's food to being late on rent. There is no drama, no one to answer to, and no one you have to check up on to make sure they paid their part of the bills or that their rent money is in.

How to Live Well on Your Own

Sometimes there can be pitfalls to living alone, and I want to share a few tips that I have to be successful.

Find Something You Can Afford

There's nothing worse than having to stretch your budget, or be stuck at home nights by yourself because you can't afford to go out. Figure out a budget that you can feasibly stick with, and then stick with it!

Pay Your Bills on Time

Mark a calendar or set reminders, whatever will work for you. There's no one else to remind you or bring it up, and the companies you owe don't like to let you know before you owe them more, plus interest. If possible, set up email reminders or emailed bills so that you have easy access and can pay them quickly with the least amount of effort. Know what will work for you to keep yourself on time and then set the right process in place so you can be successful.

Set Times to Do Housework

This was the hardest part of living on my own. It's very easy to become a hermit and never invite anyone over because it's never clean and then never clean because no one comes over. This is a vicious cycle that you want to avoid at all costs to keep yourself social and happy. Schedule time to clean in your calendar and keep with it. You can also set up weekly times for people to come over, or invite people over far in advance if you think that will help you out.

Get Connected Outside Your Space

Try joining organizations or groups that you care about, whether it has to do with your industry or even volunteering. Forcing yourself to get out of your space and be social is imperative to continuing your relationships and moving forward in life successfully.

Set More Than One Alarm

If you don't wake up, there is no one else to make sure you're up, or who might make noise in the hallways to get you up. If you have an early flight or something you can't miss, maybe ask a parent or early-rising friend to phone you in the morning to make sure you get up.

A Story

This is an embarrassing one, but I missed a flight. I actually woke up as the flight was taking off. It was a work trip, and I was only supposed to be gone for the day. I had decided to drive myself to the airport and park there because I would only be gone for six to eight hours and didn't want to make anyone drop me off and pick me up in the same day. Otherwise I probably would have woken up when someone came to the door to take me. It was a horrible feeling. Luckily, because the plane was still in the air, I was able to call, get my money back, and take the trip at a later date, but explaining that to the airline and my boss was a horrible experience that I wouldn't wish on anyone. Moral of the story—make sure you set your alarms!

CHAPTER THREE

Be Safe

Pick a place to live in a good neighborhood, or a building with a lot of safety features. It's important that you feel that you can come home at any time and feel safe.

A Story from Betsy

As mentioned earlier, when my roommate got laid off, I paid her half of the rent for a few months because it was worth it to me not to have to find another roommate. However, after a few months this stopped working, and to be honest I can't remember the exact details (as it was twenty-plus years ago!), but she moved out and I decided that I didn't want any more roommate drama. I got a smaller apartment in the same complex so I could keep my dry cleaner and my grocery store and my walking route and everything else I loved about living where I lived. And while I was not overly thrilled with the idea of being on my own, as I'm not a person that needs much "alone time" (or any, to be honest), I found that living alone is a wonderful way to get to know yourself a little better. It turned out to be quite fun! And even though I only ended up living alone for six months, I am so grateful I did, and I recommend it to everyone!

Should You Get a Pet?

The key to living alone, however, is to not get lonely. There are a few ways to remedy this, but the main way most people get around it is getting a pet.

A Story

After living on my own for a year, I was finally sick of coming home to an empty apartment every night. There was no one there to greet me, and no one happy to see my face. I weighed the different pros and cons of different types of pets, and took into account the rules of my complex. We weren't allowed to have dogs, and a cat seemed like a pretty big responsibility. I decided on a hamster, Teddy, who was the coolest hamster and a great companion for the two years he lived. It may seem silly to you that a hamster would make a difference, but after living on your own for so long, it's just nice to have another living thing around. Especially a fuzzy, cute one you can hold.

Even if you live with others, you may feel the draw to get a pet, and that is great. I think it's a wonderful idea for most people to have a pet, learn about responsibility, and care about something other than themselves. Please, however, be sure that you weigh the pros and cons of owning and caring for another living thing!

Dogs

Do you have the time to feed, walk, clean up after, and watch a dog? Are you financially set up for that kind of commitment? Do you have a living situation that is comfortable for a dog (i.e., a yard for running and a lot of space or a dog park nearby)? Will you be able to take a dog into the next living situation? For most young adults the answer to these questions is *no*.

Cats

Generally a cat would be a better choice for someone who is still planning on moving a few times in his or her life. Complexes and rental properties are generally much more accepting of cats as they aren't quite the destructive machines dogs are (I say with a loving tone). Cats are also less expensive to care for and are much lower maintenance. Again, however, make sure you are willing to commit to a cat for more than a decade and realize that you may need to turn down certain apartments and/or living situations based on extra fees (pet rent) or allergies of future roommates.

A Story

When you get a pet, it is also important to factor in whether your roommate might have/want a pet. For my sister-in-law, Taylor, and her roommate, this became a problem. Taylor had discussed getting the cat with her roommate, and they had agreed to get one. After Taylor got her cat, the roommate decided to buy a hamster. Taylor came home to her cat tormenting the poor hamster in his plastic ball. Not only was this not fair to the hamster, the roommate didn't discuss getting a hamster with Taylor at all, making her feel like her opinion didn't matter. In her next living situation, her roommate bought a fish, which Taylor's cat promptly ate. Again, not fair to the pet, and it caused a strain on the relationship.

Rodents and Birds

A step below cats on the responsibility scale, most rodents and birds are a bit cheaper and have about the same lower maintenance attraction of a cat. These types of animals are generally overlooked in most living situations and don't incur extra fees. They generally don't live as long (except for some types of birds), so the commitment of keeping them for long periods of time is diminished. Remember though, you will need to run heat and air in extreme temperature climates to keep them healthy, safe, and alive. You'll also need a pet sitter when you leave to make sure they are fed, clean, and happy. Also, choose your bird very carefully, as some are quite loud and disruptive. Bottom line: do your research!

Fish

While fish are probably the least friendly companion, they are also the easiest to care for, and, unless you want a sea salt tank with extreme fish, they are usually the cheapest pet possibility. For someone who is afraid they could kill a cactus by not watering it, I generally recommend a Beta fish. They are easy pets to care for, live on their own, and only require a small tank. They even sell slow dissolving food for Beta fish so that if you go on vacation they can eat at their normal schedule. If you have a hard time with death, however, please do not get a fish. They are fickle and do not live for long periods of time. No matter how well you care for them, sometimes it's just their time to go.

Using all these living situations and tips, we're hopeful you can find a combination that will make you happy and support your daily life. Remember when you make this decision that it will affect you every day, and having a happy place to come home to can be of utmost importance when other areas of your life are difficult. Take the appropriate steps to set yourself up for success, and then follow it up with best practices for the best living situation you could ask for.

CHEAT SHEET

- Living at home
  - Cost-effectiveness
  - Home-cooked meals
  - Convenience
  - Security
  - Support

- How to live at home successfully
  - Be respectful
  - Confront the little things
  - Go above and beyond
  - Act like an adult
  - Have fun and learn

- Living with a roommate(s)

- Reasons to live with a roommate
  - Cost-effective
  - Companionship
  - Convenience
  - Security
  - Support
  - Chores
  - Diversity

- Reasons not to live with a roommate
  - Logic
  - Habit
  - Peer pressure

- Find the right roommate
  - Rental history
  - Sleep schedule
  - Temperature comfort levels
  - Entertainment
  - Noise levels
  - Religious views
  - Lifestyle

- Chore preferences
- Personality
- Fragrance/odor sensitivity
- Allergies
- Cleanliness
- Smoking, drinking, and drugs
- Décor style

- Roommate Agreements
  - Financial responsibility
  - Living arrangements
  - Overnight guests
  - Cleaning
  - Purchases

- Be a good roommate
  - Be upfront about expectations
  - Try to say "yes" often
  - Respect your roommate
  - Stick to your word and follow through
  - Compromise
  - Clean up after yourself
  - Be aware of your roommate's sleeping habits
  - Spend quality time with your roommate
  - Lock the doors and windows when you leave
  - Be flexible with your roommate's life
  - Communicate early and often
  - Control the amount of noise you make
  - Invite your roommate out with you
  - Don't make your rules too rigid

- What to do if it doesn't work out
  - Be prepared with a plan
  - Set up a time to talk
  - Break up in person
  - Keep the discussion short
  - Be straightforward
  - Be as honest as you can

- Give notice to your roommate
- Be prepared for their reaction

- Living alone
  - Privacy
  - Freedom
  - Peace

- How to live well on your own
  - Find something you can afford
  - Pay your bills on time
  - Set times to do housework
  - Get connected outside your space
  - Set more than one alarm
  - Be safe

- Should you get a pet?
  - Dogs
  - Cats
  - Rodents and birds
  - Fish

LIVING HEALTHY

Tori

When I was in college I was not concerned at all with my health. I would be in class all day, then go to work or meetings, and then cram in homework and studying. By the time I got a chance to eat, it was never something thought out or healthy. In fact, most times it was pizza or fast food—something cheap and easy. Growing up a dancer, I was always physically active and never had to worry about what I ate. While in college I stopped dancing, and I hardly did any physical activities. Needless to say, I gained quite a bit of weight. I was unhappy, unhealthy, and didn't really know what to do to turn it around. After graduation I moved out on my own, and I really started to pay attention to what I ate. I started moving every day, including using the stairs; I lived on the fourth floor of my complex with no elevator, and had stairs in my apartment. I also started parking in the back of the parking lot. I found an exercise program that I liked and could stick to. Within a year I shed almost all of what I had gained. It was a great feeling, and I enjoyed my accomplishments, and life in general, much better!

A Story from Betsy

I have also had periods of time in my life, including during my junior year of college, when I let doing "everything else" get in the way of my health. These were times when I chose to study or work instead of exercise and paying attention to what I ate. As an obvious result, I gained weight. When this happens in my life, I acknowledge that it is a big, flashing sign that my life is not in balance;

I have to work to "right the ship" and get my health back on track. And when I do, I am always so much happier and, ironically, more productive and en route to accomplishing my goals.

Moral of these stories: if you aren't healthy, none of the rest of this book matters. You can't enjoy your career, and all of the wonderful things life offers, if you are too sick or unhealthy. If you're anything like I was, you may be overwhelmed with building your career and your new, "grown-up" life, and fitting exercise and healthy eating into your everyday routine can seem difficult. Don't stress yourself out over it! We'll walk you through tips and tricks to make it happen easily.

Your Healthy Thought

While working on this book, I had the wonderful opportunity to speak to Amy Brogan, EdD, a certified health coach and college nutrition professor (agapenutritionandfitness.com). She shared much of this chapter with me, and one of my favorite things she had to share was the "Healthy Thought." You should keep this Healthy Thought in mind while reading this entire chapter. And before we share the Healthy Thought, please keep in mind that when it comes to your health, we want you to not just think about eating and exercise, but your physical, emotional, and mental health as well. All of these are equally important to living a healthy lifestyle. If you are stressed or upset, you won't sleep well. If you indulge in too many sweets, you will feel guilty, and this will negatively impact your emotional health. All three impact each other, and it's important to find a balance among all of them.

While making changes in your daily routine toward a healthier lifestyle, remember the Healthy Thought:

Everything you put in your body or do to your body has a cumulative effect over your lifetime.

This includes the food you eat and the exercise (or lack thereof) you complete. I also like to think this includes tattoos and piercings.

Every single choice you make right now *will* have an effect on you later. The ice cream you eat every night might not be a problem now; you are young, have a high metabolism, and can work it off when you exercise tomorrow. But over time, that nightly bucket of ice cream will have a poor effect on your health.

The best way to move forward with this overall principle is to create daily habits and be consistent. Start fitting in more veggies every day via a salad before dinner and some raw vegetables for snack, or try to cut ice cream and sweets to a few times per week, or even once per week, instead of every day. Treat your body well every day, rather than abusing it and being surprised later when you are hit with health issues or injuries.

Focus on *feeling* better. This isn't just physically, but also emotionally and mentally. If you approach your lifestyle changes with the goal of looking better or losing weight, what happens when you reach your goal? Do you stop? This can also have a negative impact as you might get down on yourself for not sticking with it. *Well I'm fat anyway, so what does it matter?* Shut that voice up now! Focus on *I want to feel better every day*, and what is there to be negative about? If you make a mistake you don't have to dwell on it; just learn from it! You probably had that sweet or salty snack because it was what you wanted, and you don't have to be upset about that. What matters is doing what is good for you most of the time. You don't have to be perfect!

Make enough change, but not too much. We are big fans of baby steps! Make small changes that seem easy to you, and then it will be easy to create regular habits rather than feeling overwhelmed and stressing yourself out. You might be living on your own and find yourself sitting and watching TV most nights, as there aren't a whole lot of activities to do by yourself. This won't give you energy, or make you feel good. Try doing a few situps, squats, or pushups during the commercials. Even something as small as getting up and walking around your house or apartment during the commercial break will have a huge impact on your body over your lifetime. Remember, this is a cumulative effect!

You may start researching different fitness programs and diet plans and get overwhelmed by the pros and cons to the point where you're so confused and frustrated at all the contradictory opinions (we love the Internet, but there are a LOT of conflicting views, especially in this area) that you just throw up your hands and say "forget it!" Just remember— baby steps. Don't ever use the "there are too many programs/diets out there, I can't decide which one is best" excuse to do NOTHING! Anything small and consistent is better than nothing.

Note from Betsy: When I lived in Sacramento after I graduated from college, I didn't have many people to do things with after work once my roommate went to graduate school. Instead of waiting to be asked, I decided to reach out to some of my co-workers to see if they wanted to start walking after work. We didn't do it every day, of course, but we managed to go walking in a nearby park a few times a week. This gave me a way to become better friends with my co-workers, and I fit in some extra exercise as well! I also reached out to my high school–aged cousins who lived in town to see if they wanted to walk or do some fun exercise. This gave me a chance to get to know the two of them better, and, as a result, we are still extremely close today.

Try to make a fun change. Exercise isn't a fun word. Most people hate it. For the rest of this chapter, let's call it moving! Just move. It's that easy. It doesn't have to be at a gym, or a fitness video at home, or even boot camp. Just get up and move your body. That's it!

A Story

I hate hiking. In fact, I really hate it. I tend to think it stems from growing up with a father who loves to hike and had no sons; he forced my sister and me out on day-long hikes for miles and backpacking trips where we carried everything on our backs and changed campsites every day. One time (the last time) I agreed to go with him, I was covered in mosquito welts (much worse than bites), sunburned to a crisp, and found a tick on my stomach that had to be surgically removed when we got back home. Needless to say, being outside isn't my thing. I do love to shop, though, and I can walk around outlets all day (mostly) window shopping and spending social time with friends. Not only does this get me out and moving around, but I also get a mental and emotional break via venting frustrations with my friends.

The moral of the story: Make time daily for small changes, and every movement will have a cumulative effect on your life. There are a few strategies to help you move forward with your new Healthy Thought. Each of these strategies will help you on your road to feeling better and making the right changes for your lifestyle.

Know (and Be True to) Yourself

This may seem like a silly idea, but when it comes to making lifestyle choices, it's imperative! You know your body, your mind, the excuses you tend to make, and what you punish yourself for. You also know what you love, like, don't like, or hate. When you are making any lifestyle change, make sure it's something you know you will do, or something you know you can stick with.

I can't tell you what diet or movement plan will work for you. What works for me and what I enjoy probably won't work well for you. Make these important decisions for yourself based on what you want, not what you read in a magazine or hear from the "latest trend."

A few examples to help you figure this out:

1. If you hate to go to the gym, don't sign up for a gym membership. Find something you would enjoy doing instead, and move that way. Forcing yourself into a gym when you hate it won't help anyone. You won't be happier or feel better. Just make sure you choose something that you really will do, and find an accountability partner if you need one to stay on track.

2. If you know you will eat cookies if you keep them around the house, don't buy them. This is true for me with gummy peach rings. If they are anywhere around me, I will eat them. I went so far as to tell my husband to hide them once (and I'm ashamed to admit, I went looking for them!).

Note from Betsy: I started keeping small pieces of dark chocolate in my freezer instead of having cookies or other candy around. I eat two per day, and because they are dark chocolate and not milk chocolate, I don't ever "overindulge." I do, however, always feel like I'm having a treat!

---

3. If you will feel deprived because you didn't let yourself have those fries and you know you'll probably binge later because of it, get the fries now. Maybe just don't eat them all, or share them with someone else.

4. If you know it's hard for you to stick with an exercise program, get people to keep you accountable. My husband does this with his friends and weight lifting. They all do it together to keep each other going and encourage each other. Plus they get more time to spend together as friends, and (as a bonus) they get in shape.

5. If you know you hate working in your cubicle, see if there is a way you can use a conference room or meeting space, or ask if there is a telecommuting program so you can work from home on certain projects. This will help your mental health greatly, as you'll be happier during the workday.

6. If you're not hungry, don't eat. Listen to your body's signals and only eat when you are hungry so that you don't overeat or miss out on something you'd rather have later.

7. If you know you'll go right to the vending machine when you're hungry, pack yourself healthy snacks in advance.

Note from Betsy: The vending machine is an issue I have, as we have them EVERYWHERE around campus. I prevent myself from going too often by trying not to keep $1 bills or change around. Usually I am too embarrassed to ask for change to use the vending machine, and there isn't somewhere close to make change otherwise. The other thing I do is make sure that when I do use the vending machines, I choose baked chips or candy with peanuts so I'm making healthier choices.

The lifestyle changes that will really impact your life will be the ones that you do consistently. Try thinking about it as "tricking" yourself into being healthier. If you really know yourself and the choices you will make ahead of time, you'll be able to plan ahead and trick that little nagging voice in your head. Don't let that little voice in your head tell you what to do. Take control of your mind and body, and stick with what you really want to do.

Have a Schedule Every Day

We covered the importance of scheduling in chapter 1, but it bears repeating here. Scheduling is just as important to your health as it is to your career development. It can be as complex as a calendar blocked out or as simple as a to-do list. It can be on your phone or in a planner or little notebook you keep at all times. You know what will work for your lifestyle, so make that choice. You want to track the important items you want to get done for the day and plan for plenty of time to get all of it done.

Schedule in Rest and Relaxation

You also want to schedule time to relax, rest, and move. It may seem silly to schedule time to relax—and I have to admit, when I first heard it I thought *what a waste of time.* But you really do need to give yourself the time to enjoy your life. If you don't have time to enjoy your life, what's the point in living it? Give yourself the time to relax and rejuvenate, and your stress level will greatly decrease.

Scheduling your day and having a list of items you know you can accomplish will help you feel happier. You can physically cross (or delete) things off your list. In my opinion, writing a to-do list and crossing everything off is the best feeling in the world. It's why I still write my to-do lists on paper.

Writing down and crossing off items is also beneficial because you won't get to the end of the day thinking you didn't get anything done. I'm sure I'm not the only one who has had those days when I felt like I worked on everything but didn't really finish anything. It makes you feel as if you were busy all day but wasted the day.

> **Tip:** Make sure there are crossoffable items on your list every day! This gives you that strong sense of accomplishment that you completed tasks and that the day had purpose.

Avoid Distractions

Try to keep on track, and ignore things that will get you easily distracted. Again, know yourself. If you know you will want to check Facebook, Twitter, and Instagram every thirty minutes, try putting your phone on airplane mode or turning off the Wi-Fi on your laptop or computer. If you know you'll get sucked into a TV show, don't turn the TV on. If you know calling a friend or family member will turn into an hour-long conversation and you haven't already scheduled that in to your day, wait to call until the next day, or answer their call later.

A Story

I know that if I need to write a chapter for a book, it will take me a few hours. I need to block out a good amount of time (usually half a day) to feel as if I can really get it done and feel accomplished. I also know that I can't have access to wireless Internet, otherwise I will get sidetracked, even though it's usually helpful sidetrack items like answering clients' emails or responding to questions. I know I can't be at home, because I have pets and a husband who all, very rightly, want my attention and love. And I know I need a comfortable spot with people moving and talking, but not too loud, with music or shouting. I know I will need to have access to food and drinks but not be able to leave. Once I figured all of this out, it was easy to find a few places that fit this mold for my workspace. I am able to sit and write for hours without interruption and really feel accomplished. Plus I know I really want to work toward finishing a chapter, because finishing a chapter is my favorite feeling (besides finishing a book!).

Don't Procrastinate

This is tough for a lot of people, including me. But it is very important to keep from procrastinating to reduce stress and build your mental health. As we talked about in chapter 1, while you're building your daily schedule, plan a weekly one, and then know for the next month what your goals are. That way you can keep all your larger projects in perspective and make small steps toward finishing big projects.

A Story

I know I am awful with procrastination. And I will tell you, as I know myself, that I really do it with the best of intentions. I don't just sit and not do work, but I'll get busy working on other projects that are equally important but probably don't need to be done first. I'm especially bad with large projects. I will leave large projects to the end, knowing I can pull it out if I need to, but stressing myself out in the end. This is just another reason why I love Betsy. She is amazing at taking a large project, breaking it down into digestible pieces, and scheduling it out with time to spare. For this reason alone, she is invaluable as my coauthor. I know that if I didn't have her, I'd probably end up writing the whole thing in the final month before sending to the publisher. I completely rely on her for this, and know that I have to ask her to do this for me with any large project we work on, both for my mental health but also for her mental health when she works with me.

Note from Betsy: While I so appreciate Tori's kind words above, and I do enjoy breaking large projects into small tasks and working out a plan so we reduce all of our stress to a minimum, I (like all humans) also suffer from procrastination. Like Tori, I don't sit there and not do something, but I will sometimes let other things get in the way. Email is my biggest procrastinator-enabler, as answering email always feels "important" because somebody needs me! As discussed in chapter 1, I have a lot of email rules to help me, and most days I break at least one of them! But I also know that when I do my priority tasks first and keep my time answering email in check, everything in this chapter comes together for me, and my physical and mental health improves tremendously!

Another Note from Betsy: I'm a morning exerciser, as I know that even if I really, truly intend to exercise in the evenings, I won't. I'm just too tired at the end of the day, or my family or work will need me and I just don't seem to ever fit it in. However, if I get up and do it, even if it means getting up early, I do just fine, and really enjoy it. Figure this out for YOU, as while exercise experts might tout one time of day over another, the bottom line is that if you don't do it, it won't do any good. So do it when you can. At other times in my life I have walked with colleagues at lunchtime, as that was literally my only time to exercise. Again, just do it when you can!

A Story

My father-in-law started swimming because he wanted to find an exercising activity he could do without having to shower afterward. Why? He wanted to exercise during his lunch break, and he only had enough time for a quick exercise and not enough to "hit the showers" afterward. This soon became his routine: drive to the gym, swim for a half hour or so, dry off, change back to work clothes, and then drive back to the office. It worked for him and his schedule, and it became an easy routine to keep.

Don't Overload Your Schedule

Know your abilities and limits, and plan accordingly. Always give yourself more time than you think you'll need, and build in time to drive different places, or time for mental breaks between meetings. I try to always put a half hour between meetings and appointments to account for meetings going over, bathroom breaks, a quick stroll and stretch, and prep for the next meeting. Throwing back-to-back items in your schedule will keep you running all day and exhaust you.

Tip from Betsy: Something that will really help you in the quest to be healthy is planning. Here are some planning tips that help keep me on track. Each week as I am planning my to-do list, I include when and what I will do for exercise on my list. This gives me a check-off item that keeps me accountable and also feels good when I check it off. I also plan all of my meals (including breakfasts and lunches) in advance so I only go to the grocery store once per week. I package small bags of grapes, cherry tomatoes, cucumber slices, and carrots so they are easy to grab and pack for snacks. I eat quite a few prepackaged salads, but when I have time I make a few "homemade" salads a few at a time so I am not always starting from scratch regarding lunch prep. Bottom line: ANYTHING you can do ahead of time increases your chances of sticking with the changes you want to make.

Surround Yourself with Strong, Positive Relationships

There is a saying we like from motivational speaker Jim Rohn (even though it might be a scary one!): *You are the average of the five people you spend the most time with.* Think about that for a minute. Do a mental inventory and think about the five people you spend the most time with. It may seem silly, but do you like them? Do they have good habits? Are they what you want to be like when you "grow up"? Because if you continue spending time with them the way you are, you will be like them. Any positive or negative habits they have, you will pick up. But you may pick up negative habits much more quickly, even when you try to avoid it.

I like to use the example of you, your friend, and a chair. Think of the chair as positive behavior, and the floor as negative behavior. When you stand up on the chair and have healthy, positive habits, your friend is on the floor with negative, unhealthy habits. Now try to pull your friend up on the chair with you. It will be pretty difficult for you to do, especially if they put no effort in. Now have your friend pull you down onto the floor. Much easier, right? And you don't have much of a choice once they start pulling. It's much easier and quicker to pull someone down than pull them up. Healthy, positive habits take much more work and time, and therefore you should surround yourself with as many people who display these behaviors as possible.

So who are these people? They can be your mentors from chapter 8, family members, or anyone you think will make you better each day than the day before. They are people who you can lean on in tough times, and who will help you make better decisions. This doesn't mean you have to cut your current top five people out of your life entirely. You obviously spend time with them for a reason, and it could hurt you emotionally to remove them. Just spend a little less time with them and a lot more with other, better influencers. When you are bored and just want to chat, consider calling someone who you will have a positive, happy conversation with. Avoid calling someone who will gossip the whole time, or bring unnecessary drama to your life.

Note from Betsy: After reading this, you might decide that you need to shrink someone's involvement in your life. This might not be easy for you. Perhaps this person has been in your life for a while, or perhaps it's a family member. At the end of the day, this is all about you and your success, so please do what is best for you. This person will survive. You have to protect yourself. Most people find it easier to gradually taper folks off instead of cutting them out "cold turkey." Perhaps take longer to return phone calls or texts. Maybe only accept every third or fourth invitation to see them. Relationships ebb and flow over time, so this transition will probably not seem unnatural to the person whose impact you are shrinking.

The Golden Rule

We love the Golden Rule! The best way to keep your mind healthy and happy is to treat others well. Think about what kind of person you want to be, and then treat others in a way that displays that persona. When people see your actions, they will talk you up to others and build your reputation (brand). You'll be surprised at the amount of influence you will have if you respect and honor others. People will be more drawn to you and want you to be in their top five circle. Plus, you'll feel like a better person and reduce drama and stress in your life.

Treat others well, even if they aren't in the room. If you're talking about someone, ask yourself, *Would this embarrass them if they walked in the room right now?* If it would, stop, as this is a clue that it doesn't need to be said. If you do say it, you are creating your own drama. You never know when someone will walk around a corner, or if your words will reach their ears. As a species we love to talk about each other and even gang up on the weak at times. Try to avoid this behavior and keep everyone in your life, including yourself, happy.

A Story

Betsy's friend, a college professor, was walking down the hall to teach her class when she heard one of her students talking about her class. They weren't positive words, and when the student saw her, the student started trying to play it off as if she was talking about something else, or it wasn't a big deal. The student was mortified! She hid in the back of the class for the rest of the semester, and she rarely ever spoke to the professor again. That student created her own drama and caused stress and anxiety in her life for no reason. (And it didn't make the professor's day either!)

The best thing you can do for your mental health is to decrease your stress and stay away from drama—especially creating your own. I promise you'll have plenty of grown-up drama without creating your own!

Try New Things

There are always new advances in healthy living. Don't let yourself get in a rut. Be willing to try new things, and even pull in a group of friends, or your family, to try it with you and make it fun. If you make experimenting with your health a social event, like hosting a healthy potluck or getting a group together to play flag football or join a softball league, it will be more fun. It's important to steer clear from making anything in this chapter a chore. Make living healthy something you enjoy and want to do more often, so it's easier for you.

Mentally, you can try new experiences, workspaces, or friends to keep your mind healthy and fresh. Learn to knit, or paint, or dance, or maybe even try flying lessons. Go bungee jumping. If you are afraid of heights, go get a new type of massage. Do anything to widen your horizons and give you a new outlook on something.

Nutritionally, you can try new foods and experiment with different ways of cooking and eating that you enjoy. Be willing to find new, healthy foods that you might like (or retry some you hated as a kid), and learn new, good choices that you didn't even know existed.

Physically, you can try moving new ways or at different times of the day/different days of the week. Try going to a trampoline park, or go rock climbing, or join an Ultimate Frisbee team. Find new ways to get your body moving doing something you like, and always look for new things that you enjoy. Then, if you've always exercised in the morning, try adding in a walk after dinner, or taking a nighttime dance class by yourself or with your significant other. You might find that it helps you wind down and end the day on a happy note.

As you experiment, you will find things you don't like, probably more often than not. Keep at it! You never know when a food allergy or injury will surface later in life and impact the way you like to live your life (e.g., a gluten allergy or knee injury that greatly impacts your diet or exercise routine). If you're always looking for new ways to enjoy your healthy lifestyle, it will be easy to make adjustments when life gets in the way. This shouldn't be something you have to do, but something you enjoy doing because it makes you feel better!

Check Your Food

Don't ever take someone's word for it. Learn about the food you are putting in your body. Even well-meaning people can lead you astray. Amy mentioned she'd heard people say that bacon is protein, so it's a healthy breakfast choice. This is not true; bacon has a lot of fat and is not good for you. She also heard someone say that Pop Tarts have real fruit in them, so therefore they are good for you. Whether these people actually believe what they are saying or are just trying to appease their guilt for eating poorly, they are wrong. As a society, we trust what our friends and family tell us, take it at face value, and don't investigate. (This, of course, is probably because we want to believe that bacon is good for us!)

> **Tip:** Be honest with yourself. You usually know intuitively whether a food is good or bad. Don't trick yourself into thinking things are healthy just because you want to eat them.

Take the time to read nutrition labels and know what you are eating. And when you have time, go beyond the nutrition label. Most people don't even know what half the things on a nutrition label are. Look up what is in your food and take the time to consider if you can make healthier choices.

Limit Processed Foods

Processed food is better known as convenience food, which, while you were a student, you were probably well versed in when you didn't have a full kitchen to make a meal. The basic idea is to eat fresh. If you eat an orange, you know what is in the orange. It isn't processed.

While speaking with Amy, she gave me the best tip I've heard in a long time: Shop on the outside edges of the grocery store. Trying to always think about whether food is processed and/or good for you can be exhausting, but a great way to keep your food simple is to stay on the outer edges of the grocery store and avoid the middle aisles. The outside is generally where the fresher food is kept, including vegetables, fruit, and meat.

Move Every Day

It is essential for you to move several times a day, every day. This can be as challenging as running in the mornings or as easy as getting up from your desk every hour for a quick stroll and stretch. Especially for those who work at a desk all day, it can be dangerous to your health to lean over a keyboard nonstop for hours on end.

You don't always have to move for long periods of time. If you don't do anything now and don't want to commit to a rigorous program, literally just move for ten minutes a day. Walking is a very easy way to do this. Walk around your block, take a stroll down the street during your lunch break, park at the far side of the parking lot, take the stairs instead of the elevator, or even walk around your office. If you're at home, take your dog for a walk or get up and move around the house during TV commercials. Anything is better than nothing, and you don't have to set aside a long time every day to do it. Break up your moving, and plan to do it between your appointments or before or after a big meeting to blow off adrenaline. I like to pace during phone meetings and walk around my house (cell phone signal permitting!).

The best thing you can do today is to just think about it. Before you settle on the couch for the night, make the mental decision to do something. Because once you sit on that couch and sink into the cushions, it will be that much harder for you to get up.

Balance Your Diet

The rules haven't changed; you should always try to have protein, carbs, and fat, as well as fruits and vegetables, in most meals to keep your diet balanced. But let's be realistic. That doesn't always happen. We're busy, and there are times when you just grab a quick bagel for lunch or a side of fries as a snack. That doesn't mean you've blown the whole day and done a horrible thing; it means you're human and have a real life.

When you can't balance every meal, try to think about balancing your daily meals. If you had that bagel at lunch, you know you should have more protein at dinner and avoid the carbs. If you have a really carb-heavy day, try to get more protein and vegetables in the next day. Keep your recent meals in the back of your mind as you make your food decisions, and then you can make healthier choices.

This also counts for when you are having cravings. If you *really* want that chocolate, give it to yourself. Don't deprive yourself, because then you won't be able to stick with your healthy lifestyle plan. Just don't eat the entire box; have a very little bit and balance it with something healthy later. Easy, right? When you're more satisfied, you'll eat less. You'll be happier, and then feel better.

Sleep

As a college student, I know I rarely slept. I'm still someone who doesn't require a whole lot of sleep, so this is another challenging strategy for me. But sleep cannot be underestimated! Without sleep you can't function the way you need to. You'll be tired, won't be fresh to take on your schedule for the day, and will be less productive. This will cause more stress later, and then less sleep. It's a vicious cycle you need to steer clear of, so make sure you schedule in plenty of sleep.

Make Trades Where You Can

This is one of my favorite strategies because it really lets you personalize your healthy lifestyle. When you get to know yourself really well, you'll know what you can and can't live without. Make the cuts where you can, and especially where you don't notice. Let's say you like to have mayonnaise on every sandwich. If you can make the switch to a lower fat option, without suffering a huge loss, then do so. If you must have that full-fat mayonnaise, try a cut somewhere else. Or you could even try a healthier option. I've used plain Greek yogurt instead of mayonnaise or sour cream in a lot of recipes because I can't tell the difference and the Greek yogurt is much better for me. If you can severely diminish your sweets because you want your salty snacks, do so. Make the choices that will make you happy and you will stick with it.

With all of these strategies, you will be ready to take on your new healthy lifestyle and move forward toward a happy, feel-good, long life. Always remember that every small choice will have a large impact later on, and not to take any decision lightly. Make the small steps that you know you can stick with, and enjoy it!

CHEAT SHEET

- Your Healthy Thought

- Know (and be true to) yourself

- Have a schedule every day
  - Schedule in rest and relaxation
  - Avoid distractions
  - Don't procrastinate
  - Don't overload your schedule

- Surround yourself with strong, positive relationships

- The Golden Rule

- Try new things

- Check your food

- Limit processed foods

- Move every day

- Balance your diet

- Sleep

- Make trades where you can

Source: Amy Brogan, EdD, Certified health coach/college nutrition professor, www.agapenutritionandfitness.com

FAMILY, FRIENDS, AND LOVE
Tori

There are a lot of transitions you go through as you make the shift from full-time student to full-time adult after you graduate from college. You experience a lot of strange feelings; it is the end of an era. Relationships are a huge factor in this, as you may be used to dealing with certain people, or certain types of people, all around your age. Once you are a graduate and are out on your own, you may experience some emotional whiplash. The tough moments will be not having those long winter and summer breaks, and watching some of your friends go back to school in the fall without you, or moving to a different city or state or country.

It's definitely a bittersweet feeling. And if you don't like change it can be a very difficult transition. You've been going to school every year since before you can remember, picking out your school supplies, getting textbooks, and meeting new teachers and peers. You'll now have a completely different life experience, but it can be so much more fun! In this chapter, we're going to walk you through how to build and maintain your relationships during the transition.

Grown-Up Life Is Different

If you didn't feel like an adult when you turned eighteen, you're definitely one now! But before we discuss how to cope with the postcollege transition, we'd like to cover *why* grown-up life is so different.

When I graduated I wasn't really sure what to expect. There was mystery to life after college. When people asked what I was going to do, I knew

I was moving and starting the new job, but had a hard time seeing past those two things. It took a few months to get used to life postschool, and I swear I'm still in the transition of growing up, but I promise it gets easier!

Here are the top postcollege life changes you'll experience that impact your relationships:

More "You" Time

You're not surrounded by other students in a dorm, fraternity/sorority, or student housing anymore. The social buffer of always having someone around is pretty much gone. You might have a roommate or two, but at best you might have a few other people your age living around you. You probably go to work every weekday, and most likely have to be at work early, so you won't be going out late with your friends as often anymore. As we mentioned in chapter 3, you'll most likely be spending many more nights on the couch on your own. With this added "you" time, it can be difficult to motivate yourself to go out on your own and meet new people.

You'll also have more time to think and really learn more about how you prefer to live when you have the choice. You'll have time to read books, cook more, and find what lifestyle suits you best.

A Story from Betsy

I remember so clearly the dinner my roommate and I had with a friend from high school shortly after college graduation. This friend was older and had been out of college and on his own for more than a year, with a pretty nice "grown-up" job in his field. He tried to explain how much free time he now had since he wasn't in school anymore, and that it was a challenge at first to figure out what to do with it. I didn't understand (at all) what he meant, but soon I realized what he was talking about, and I had to go through my own transition regarding what to do with this time that was all mine to spend.

More Sleep

No more late-night cramming sessions or papers to drive you crazy. You'll most likely be coming home from work at a reasonable hour and leaving early in the morning, so if you are used to staying up until 6 a.m., things are going to need to change! Your body will adjust to your new sleep schedule and, hopefully, you'll be getting more sleep than you did in college. As we discussed in chapter 4, more sleep leads to a happier, healthier you.

You're the Rookie

You may have been the "big dog" on campus and enjoyed knowing your surroundings, the rules of your campus, and where everything was. Suddenly, you're not just surrounded by freshmen through seniors. You're in a work environment with co-workers who are all kinds of ages and have many types of accomplishments. You're the newbie, and it will take a while to feel comfortable in your new role. There will also be a heightened sense of competition, especially if you were used to doing very well in school. You and your friends will all find different types of jobs at different companies and have very different salaries. We'll talk more about your career and how to keep your career momentum going in chapter 7.

You're Judged as a Grown-Up

Remember when you were in school, how it was OK to miss work if you had a school assignment or finals, and people usually gave you the benefit of the doubt because you were young and still learning the ways of the world? Those days are over. You are a real adult now, and people will judge you as such. The days of being the rambunctious, risk-taking, bad-mouthing college kid may be over now. You're going to be around older, more mature people.

You will be compared to others around you and want to make sure you compose yourself well; keep yourself professional, ambitious, and happy. No one wants to work or spend time with someone who is stuck in their youth years.

A Story

I'm not sure how much this story applies to the content of the book, but it is definitely a growing up story—and one of my favorites—so I have to share it. The year my sister, CJ, turned eighteen years old, we piled a bunch of friends into a car and made the road trip down to Disneyland to celebrate for a weekend. We decorated her car with "Disneyland or Bust!" "Happy Birthday!" and "She's 18!" We made the drive down safely and were ecstatic to start our fun weekend in the park. And the first day was great, until about halfway through when CJ noticed that she was missing her keys. We decided not to panic, because we knew they had to be in the park somewhere; we had driven there that morning. We split into groups to find lost-and-found areas and anyone who could help us.

An hour later, with no luck, we went back to the car, thinking that she may have dropped the keys by the car itself. We were surprised to find the keys locked in the car, with the car running. She had left the car running for six hours! While we were trying to call someone to get into the car for her, a Disney parking security guard pulled up on his Segway, radioed to his co-workers, and soon we were surrounded by golf carts and Disney security. They had all been watching the car the entire day, wondering who the birthday girl was that had left the car running with the keys locked inside. They had to meet her! They helped us get into the car, at no cost to us, and then gave her a birthday sticker to make her feel better. CJ swore it would be her last stupid mistake as a child, because she was an adult now, after all.

Stress about Money

We talked about this in chapter 2, but just to reiterate, you may have been on a budget in college and now it will completely change. Most likely any financial help you had from parents, family, or financial aid will be gone. You are now in control of your money and need to know how you want and need to spend it. The roof over your head, food in your belly, and toilet paper in your bathroom are more important than booze and video games. After college, nobody is divvying up your finances for you, and you'll become more aware of how pricey all the fun things you love to do are. This can affect your relationship with friends, boyfriends, and family, as you may need to sit some activities out or reassess how you spend time with people.

Coping with These Changes

Once you've realized that these are some of the big-ticket changes you can expect, now it will be easier to deal with them. This doesn't mean life as you know it is over. It means that you have an opportunity to grow and develop yourself as an adult. You can still go to parties and hang out with your friends, and you will (undoubtedly) make stupid decisions. It's all a part of growing up. We don't expect you to be perfect, but we want to give you the tools to be as successful as you can. These are all things I wish someone had told me when I was graduating, and it may have helped me in my transition to adulthood.

A Story

I had a very difficult postcollege transition. Much of it was brought on myself, because I decided to move three hours away from all of my college friends, the people I knew and where I had been very successful. I worked from home, and it was very hard to make new friends or branch out. I broke up with my boyfriend of more than four years, someone I had been dating since high school. And I really had no idea what to expect out of postcollege life. I got very lonely, and wasn't really sure what to do about it. I started considering moving again, just to change my surroundings and give myself a fresh outlook. And while moving away seemed like a good idea at the time, I'm very happy I stuck with my location and job, because my life would be very different had I moved. And in that loneliness I found the time to write when I was alone, and I wrote the proposal for our first book. You never know what can come from your difficult times, so try to stick with it, learn from the tough times, and move forward. As Dory said in the movie *Finding Nemo*, "Just keep swimming!"

Family

We'll start with family. We talked a little about dealing with family postcollege in chapter 3, but that really only applied if you lived at home. What if you move back to their area, or move even farther away? You can still expect your parents to think of you as "their baby" and, in many cases, still try to take care of you. You might still be sitting at the kids' table at

Thanksgiving (especially if you are not married), and they'll tell you when to put your jacket on and probably second-guess many of your relationship and career changes.

I went to college a few hours' drive away from my parents' house, and I talked to them a few days a week to check in. I was used to living on my own, making my own decisions, and dealing with problems. My college apartment wasn't in the safest location, and a few robberies would happen every once in a while, but I knew how to stay safe and was fine being an adult and taking care of myself. After graduation I moved within fifteen minutes of my parents' house, and I was in contact with my parents a lot more often. My mom would call and get worried if I didn't answer. This hadn't happened while I was away at college, so I asked her why she would get worried when I only lived fifteen minutes away. She seemed to think it was because I was closer and in her area to take care of—plus my little sister had moved much farther away to attend college after I graduated. It took some time to grow accustomed to being back in the realm of my parents, even though I paid my own rent, had my own apartment, and worked full time. Parents will always be parents, but the way you treat your parents will change as you grow up and mature into an adult.

Listen, Follow Your Gut, and Learn

Your parents (most likely) really want the best for you, but sometimes it can be hard for them to let go and let you live your own life. Unfortunately, some mistakes you need to make on your own to learn. What happened to your parents may not necessarily happen to you. You have your own life to live and therefore need to make the choices that you think are appropriate for you. That being said, I don't mean you should ignore everything your parents say. They have had much more life experience than you, and they do know you very well. So please take what your parents say into consideration, balance their suggestions with what your "gut" is telling you to do, and try to make the decision that will work for the life you want to build.

Mutual Respect

If you're still talking back or throwing tantrums with your parents, you will always be treated like a child. In other words, if you act like a child, they'll treat you like one. Finding a mutual respect with your parents is key to finding a relationship that works. Respect can be shown in a myriad of ways, but I'll share some of what I've noticed.

Acknowledge and Thank Your Parents for Everything

This can be as small as taking you to lunch or as big as including you in a vacation or trip. Notice how their eyes will light up, and they'll be even happier doing something for you because you have shown that you appreciate it.

Treat Them How You Want to Be Treated

It's the Golden Rule—again! Think about when you may have kids one day. How would you want them to treat you? I can bet that it won't be by talking back, ignoring them, or fighting often. Try to keep the Golden Rule in mind when you interact with your parents, and it will come across in your actions. (P.S. These are the grandparents of your future kids, which is probably the subject for a whole different book, but it's always good to keep the big picture of your life in perspective!)

Discuss Your Problems

No one's life is perfect. The more you are open to sharing your issues with your parents, the more respect they will have for you, because you recognize the fact that you need help. They won't laugh at you or make you feel stupid but rather be happy that you shared with them so they can help you through it. They are your parents, after all. If you feel as if they aren't taking you seriously or aren't listening, try a different approach with them. Speak calmly and think out what you want to say and get from the conversation prior to having it. Avoid arguments and act like an adult. You'll be surprised by the amount of respect that can come from these types of conversations.

Apologize

Every time you have an argument, or if you said or did something you shouldn't have, say you're sorry. Showing you are mature enough to realize you've done something wrong, even if there was wrong done on both sides, will go a long way in showing respect and gaining it back from your parents.

Be Helpful

Always ask how you can help your parents. Go out of your way to do something nice for them, or help them with a task they can't do on their own. Not only will they be appreciative but also they'll be more willing to help you when you need it (think moving to a new apartment, needing handyman help, etc.). It will show your respect for your parents and gain more respect from them in turn.

Say "I Love You"

And say it often! Share with your parents how you feel, let them know you love them, and they will show it back. Be affectionate with hugs and kisses, and show your parents that you are a loving person. It doesn't cost you anything, and it will mean a lot to them.

Include Your Parents in Your Life

Talk to them regularly, visit them often, and include them in activities. Take them to the movies or for a picnic. Take them to the park you loved as a kid, go on a hike, or spend the day shopping with them. Your time means a lot to your parents, so when you can give it, please do!

Graduating from the Kids' Table

After you've built this mutual respect with your parents, it should be easier for them to see you as an adult. They will always have advice for you, but including you in adult activities and handing you that glass of wine will seem much easier when you don't look twelve in their mind's eye. If you're still getting placed with the kids at holidays (and keep in mind sometimes you may have to, if there isn't enough room), try having an open and honest conversation with your parents about how it makes you feel to sit with children. They may have just not noticed you were upset, and it will be an easy change.

Do keep in mind the timing of having such a conversation, though; if you approach your mother about being displeased with your location at the kids' table as she's trying to put the finishing touches on the Thanksgiving turkey while the stuffing is burning and the potatoes haven't even been mashed yet, you're more likely to get a "we all have to make sacrifices, life isn't fair" response.

Accepting or Dodging Tough Questions

The dreaded "why aren't you married yet?" question is just one of several questions that can make you feel small and insignificant, especially when surrounded by family and those you love. Other questions can include when your career will pick up, why you're taking a break from work (if you hated your job and had to move on—we'll discuss the right way to do that in chapter 7), when you'll get a boyfriend or girlfriend, when you'll have kids, and much, much more. Family knows how to push buttons, and you might think it's their job to push them! Many times, the questioner is simply trying to disarm you, poke fun, or embarrass you. They may even simply be trying to find a way to relate to you and show they care. Regardless, it can definitely be annoying. You'll always have uncomfortable questions asked of you, and so it's important to find the adult way to respond.

Tip: Throwing a tantrum, storming out, or being passive aggressive are all bad ideas! Remain cheerful and try to find a mature way to blow it off. Try to remember not to take it personally, and remember that they are probably trying to get attention just for asking it— especially if they ask it around a group.

Brainstorm "good" answers, like "Can you repeat that?" This works well for outrageous questions and usually redirects the conversation. Other good answers include:

- "Gosh, I don't have an answer today."

- "Wow, that's kind of personal. Let's talk about something else."

- "How would you feel if I asked you something similar?"

Verbal Sleight of Hand

Completely avoid answering the question by deflecting a question back. This can't always work, but if you don't know the relative well you can attempt avoidance. You can try throwing a related question back at them, like asking how old they were when they were married. Or you can simply ignore it and ask them another question. No one will judge you for not wanting to answer the dreaded holiday questions.

Tell Them What They Want to Hear

If your aunt is simply being protective and wants to know when you'll settle down, tell her you haven't found anyone good enough for you yet, but that you're sure he's coming around the corner. If your uncle is poking fun at you, tell him it's because you have no idea how to date or that none of the supermodels have returned your calls, and so you'll probably die alone, with cats. This might keep them from asking these goofy questions, and it keeps you in control of the conversation.

Disarm the Questioner with Humor

Try asking your grandma which boyfriend or girlfriend you should choose, because you have so many. Or say that you've always been a hermit and were looking into buying a cave. Smile and shrug it off, and you'll look happier and your family will feel comfortable laughing with you.

All in all, try to remain positive and not be hurt by your family's invasiveness. They love you and want to be included and understand you better. Be comfortable with who you are and the decisions you make, and it will be easier to take on the questions from family. Be thankful and optimistic about the life you lead.

Enjoy the New Family Dynamic

You, your parents, and your brothers and sisters are all shifting into a new dynamic when you graduate from college. Enjoy this change and try to learn as much as you can. If you've had brothers and sisters go through it before you, you can learn from what they did well (especially since you have both sides of the story from your sibling(s) and parents). If you're the oldest, like me, you'll go through the transition again when your younger sibling(s) graduate. Remember that change is good, and you just have to find ways to make the change work. You may have to put more effort into your relationships, but they will continue to grow and flourish.

Friends

When you're in college, you're surrounded by people your age, and it's easy to make a lot of friends. After college it will be harder to keep these relationships healthy, and you'll have to put much more effort into meeting new people. You'll also have different standards of living based on different salaries, and so you will have to make plans based on the lowest common denominator of salary. There is much more to think about!

If You're Far Away

It's a given that when you graduate from college, either you or your friends will move. It's very rare for you to all stay in the same location. You'll get job offers from everywhere and have to make the right career moves. Long-distance friendships mean planning time to visit each other and making the effort to call or text regularly enough to keep your friendships strong.

A Story

I have the unlucky position of not having any of my high school or college friends live near me. People moved across the state, and most of my friends live six hours away (including my sister). This makes it very difficult to have regular plans with my friends, and I try to plan weekends away or weekends for them to come visit. This means getting all my work and chores done during the week and making time for my friends. It can also be more expensive as you have travel costs when friends live far away. I make it work though, and we always have a lot of fun when we can enjoy each other's company. We just have to plan ahead!

A Story from Betsy

When I graduated from college, I moved three hours away from my college town. This was both a blessing and a curse, as I was still close enough to visit but far enough away that visiting did take

111

some effort. I had many friends still in school and many others who stayed in our college town, and I found myself going back almost every weekend. This was fine, at first, but I soon realized that I was not "connecting" with my new city, and I was feeling quite torn between my two "homes." I didn't feel as if I belonged in either place. This is not something I would recommend. Wherever you move, commit to making that your home. Stay there on the weekends. Embrace your new community.

If You're Close

If you're lucky and live near some of your friends after graduating, you will still need to put more effort in than you used to. We briefly touched on this at the beginning of the chapter; there isn't a social buffer anymore. There are no longer parties that everyone is invited to, and you aren't running into people at the library or at Starbucks all the time. You'll need to make the conscious effort to create plans and make time for each other outside of work, family activities, and significant others.

A Story

When CJ was in college, it was really easy for her to hang out with friends and make time for them, especially with those who were in the same major program at her school. None of them had full-time jobs, and so they would spend time together right after class. They all lived within twenty minutes of each other and could carpool when needed. Postgraduation, though, posed many more challenges. She kept two main friends, one of whom moved an hour-and-a-half away, and the other entered law school. She discovered that compromise was necessary, and that she couldn't be sensitive if plans fell through. More often than not, one of them would have to drive far to meet the other, or plans would be canceled at the last minute because of work obligations. As long as they all made the effort to keep in touch, either through text messages or social media, she knew the friendships would last. CJ and her friends would let each other know when great things happened in their lives, and they still made time for important events in each other's lives. She and her friends decided that friendships after college are much more about the quality of the time you spend together, not the quantity.

Making New Friends

If your experience is anything like mine, you may move to a new city where you don't know anyone. Or you may stay put and everyone else around you moves away. Regardless, it can be very tough to make new friends. You aren't surrounded by people your age, or even with people who have similar interests, and you'll need to put yourself out there. Your schedule will seem to fill to the brim, and pressures and stress will make you wish you could just go to sleep. Don't! Follow some of these tips to put yourself out there and make new friends after college:

Join a Professional Organization

Not only will this help your career, but you can meet people who love what you love to do. Professional organizations usually have local chapters, and so you can find people around you who do similar things for work. If nothing else, you can learn more about your industry and vent to others who understand what you go through at work.

A Story from Betsy

Everywhere I have lived I've quickly become involved in the local professional organizations as a way to meet people, expand my network, and (bonus!) grow as a professional. This strategy has helped me become "anchored" in three different cities. If I ever move again, you can bet I'll employ this same strategy!

Another Story from Betsy

My closest friends are my best friends from high school, a friend I met though a professional organization, friends I met through teaching, and a friend I met because our daughters went to pre-school together. The poem, "Make new friends, but keep the old; one is silver and the other gold" couldn't be more true. Friends come from all areas of your life, as long as you are open to it!

Join a Sports League

This has the added benefit of getting exercise! You'll also meet people who like to be active like you. This can be anything from Ultimate Frisbee to bowling or softball. Find a group that you want to join and stick with it. You can ask if anyone wants to grab dinner after, and grow friendships.

Volunteer

Find a cause you care about and donate your time. Not only will you be helping others, you'll be helping yourself! It will feel good, and you can find other people who care about what you care about. This passion will give you a quick bond and help you develop long-lasting friendships.

Go to Church

Join a small group for recent college graduates. Find a church that you like and ask about any groups or activities they have for someone your age. Then you can meet many others who share your beliefs and join in the regular activities. Maybe you can even get more involved and start a group or host some activities!

Take Classes That Interest You

A fantastic way to find these classes is through local coupon sites, such as Groupon or LivingSocial. Sign up for their email lists and buy and attend classes that seem of interest to you. This can be cooking classes, dance classes, pottery classes, boot camp, or anything that seems fun to you. You can even find some classes at a local community college that might help you develop your career or understand more about something you've always been interested in. You're used to being in school, so the benefits here should be obvious. You'll be sitting next to someone, so be sure to strike up a conversation and offer to study together or hang out after class.

Use Websites to Meet People with Similar Interests

Some sites will help you meet groups of people with interests in everything from hiking to social media to music. Meeting these groups of people with your same interests can help you narrow down your friend field, and regular attendance will get you out of your house and around people you like.

While all of this may seem difficult, or at the very least a lot of work, you should appreciate the fact that these new friendships may be based more on interests than any of your past friendships (most friendships growing up are out of necessity and proximity in classes or neighbors). As you grow older, you learn more about yourself and can surround yourself with people you really like and who truly appreciate how amazing you are. It will take more effort, but the rewards will be exponential!

When One of You Makes More Money

This can be a delicate situation, and one you want to tread carefully—especially if you make more than your friend. You were used to both being on tight budgets in college, but your friend could end up having a much higher starting salary than you, or you than them, often for the simple reason that you chose different industries with different pay scales. You'll need to adjust your friendship accordingly.

If you make more, be aware that what doesn't seem like an expensive dinner to you may be your friend's food budget for the week. Or a trip you really want to take may have to wait so your friend can have time to save up for it. This may not seem fair, but you are their friend and they need your grace and kindness. You never know when the tables might turn and you will make less. You'd want them to treat you just as well, so keep that in mind.

If it's your friend that makes more, try to be as honest as possible about what you can and can't afford and what your limits are. It's always an uncomfortable discussion, but you might be pleasantly surprised when they say, "You know, I really can't afford it either." They may have just not wanted to let you down. He/she is your friend, after all, so be upfront with activities that you think would be fun and in your budget.

This also applies if one of you is unemployed. Being unemployed is an awful experience, but it's made worse when a friend wants to go out and leaves you because you can't afford it. Try to feel for the other person and what they are going through. Offer to take them to a "freedom dinner," or something fun, where you foot the bill and celebrate the fact that they are making a change in their life. When they are hired, celebrate again! Enjoy every step of the journey and do your best to help less fortunate friends enjoy it, too. Free activities are also good, of course. The goal is to get together and enjoy each other's company, after all!

Love

Love is probably the hardest transition after college, and so we saved it for last. Chances are you've had a relationship or two in college, and once you graduate you have some very difficult decisions to make.

CHAPTER FIVE

Continuing Your Relationship

Just as we discussed how friendships are hard to maintain after college, your romantic relationship will probably be harder. There are a slew of new challenges in your way that you haven't had to deal with before. The social buffer of always going to parties together fades, you could be surrounded by young, attractive co-workers (or even a guy or gal a few years older who is endearingly showing you the ropes at work), or your boyfriend or girlfriend may not choose a compatible career postcollege. And these changes will make things very challenging very quickly.

You're also going through a lot of changes yourself—discovering the lifestyle you want, the choices you want to make, and starting to plan the rest of your life how you want it. You may not agree on some big lifestyle choices. If one of you wants to continue going to school, it can put a huge financial hardship on the other. Or you might decide to live together out of financial necessity, which can cause more friction between you or a potentially disapproving family. The possibilities for "drama" are endless. Bottom line: you will probably have more grown-up stresses and problems than you did in your carefree college days.

A Story

When CJ graduated, she and her boyfriend were about to celebrate their three-year anniversary. They decided that they wanted to continue dating and try to adjust to the new postcollege lifestyles. It was not an easy transition. CJ was extremely stressed for the first few weeks while she juggled graduating, moving into a new place, and starting her new job. At the same time, her boyfriend was trying to get approved for a full-time job and help CJ out financially during her transition by covering some of her meals. CJ and her boyfriend had become accustomed to hanging out almost every day and taking spontaneous trips, which no longer fit into their schedules or budget.

Their schedules even became somewhat opposite—he had two weekdays off and she had weekends off. They fought and argued on occasion about things that didn't really matter, but after several weeks the relationship adapted. They optimized the times when they could be together, and they decided that any time they were able to spend together was better than nothing at all. In fact, it seemed better after college because they now have more to talk about because of their different jobs, and they grow closer together as they grow their careers. They continue to try to be the best support system possible for each other.

Long-Distance Relationships

At best, you and your significant other will live close to each other and be able to spend time together often. At worst, you'll be offered jobs in different locations and have to decide between one of you giving up your dream career or having a long-distance relationship. Many of the tips provided under maintaining friendships will apply and help you in your postcollege relationship, but if you decide long distance is your best option, there are some additional tips that can help you manage.

Note: Before you decide to embark on a long-distance relationship, please think long and hard about it. And talk to others who have successfully and unsuccessfully had them. Relationships thrive and grow through the little day-to-day experiences as well as the fabulous shared weekends and vacations. Long-distance relationships work beautifully (and sometimes permanently) for some, but for most people, having their loved one close is really important. Just think about it.

Be Upfront

Establish guidelines for your new relationship, and decide on what you both can commit to. This will help you know what to expect from each other and will keep you happier longer. Will you have online video dates? Will you call every night? Or maybe you think a few times per week is enough. How do you feel about spending time with the opposite sex? Decide what guidelines will work best for you and your partner, and then stick with them.

Be Honest

Once you have that plan, it may not always work as well as you had hoped. Let each other know and communicate openly with each other.

You can always make changes to your relationship rules to find what will work best for you. The important thing is to be honest with yourself and with each other so you can make these decisions together with the least amount of fighting possible.

Be Faithful

This seems obvious, but it can be difficult when you aren't around the person you love. Avoid temptation and speak with your partner often so you feel connected with him or her. (And if you feel you can't be faithful, do the right thing and break up first. Be a grown-up.)

Be Realistic

Sometimes the logistics of a long-distance relationship can be difficult. Know your limits and what will and won't work for you. If it's not working, maybe this isn't something you can do. Reconsider a career move and moving closer, or reconsider the relationship.

Ending Your Relationship

If you are sure it just won't work out after college, and you want to enter the next phase of your life on your own, ending the relationship can be tough. Make a clean break and move forward with a positive attitude. If you second-guess yourself and move back, it can only cause more heartbreak. Remember that you ended the relationship for a reason, and keep yourself open for meeting new people.

A Story

I dated the same guy from my senior year of high school through college. The last semester of college I had an Aha! moment about this relationship, and I realized we weren't really compatible in the long run. We were from different countries and cultures, and had completely different ideas of how to live our lives. I had a discussion with him about the compromises we would both have to make, but it didn't seem as if we were getting anywhere. I wanted to move back to my home area, and he wanted to stay to continue school. Neither of us was willing to budge, and so we ended our relationship. I was heartbroken, but it was the right thing to do. I am so much happier now because I was able to live my life the way I wanted without having to make compromises for anyone else.

Having a breakup talk is always difficult. Do it in person and come prepared with the main points you want to get across. Stick with "I feel" statements, rather than accusing the other person and stirring up further discussions and arguments; it's not the time or place to have a drawn-out argument. Be very clear about the outcome and what you expect from the other person postbreakup. Do you want to cut communication completely? Do you expect to meet up within a week to return each other's things? How will you treat mutual friends?

Meeting New People (Love)

We talked about meeting new people and different ways to do it when you want to make friends, and this can all be applied to meeting a new person in the interest of a relationship. There are a few additional ways to meet people, however, and there are probably some rules you want to follow.

Office Romances

This is a common way to meet potential love interests when you are a full-time adult. You will be working in an office with people, hopefully around your age, and it will seem easy to strike up a relationship because you are around the person often. This can also be dangerous depending on your working relationship (e.g., if you are attracted to your boss) or the rules of your organization. Make sure that you review any rules before getting involved, as a new relationship is not worth the career you've spent years building, no matter how cute he or she is.

Work-related romances might not be in the same office, and this is something to research as well. What are the rules about dating customers or vendors? Be very clear who is off limits (and who isn't).

Going Out

Going out with friends after work or on the weekends will introduce you to many new people. This can be a fun way to socialize and meet love interests. If you decide to go out drinking, make sure you have a sober friend around at all times to keep an eye on you (and drive you home!). Alcohol can lead to poor decisions, and you don't want to have to regret anything later. Have a group with you so that you can easily retreat back to your friends if someone starts to act a little bit crazy or scares you.

Online Dating

The statistics for how many marriages were built out of online dating are rising. It seems more and more people are meeting online, and it can be a great way to meet people! You don't have to worry about awkward social pauses, as you really get to know the person before there is any physical activity, and you have a great way to screen people you don't really care to meet. The pitfall of online dating, however, is what has become known as catfishing. This is where someone lies about who they really are and uses a fake persona to get close to other people. This can be as simple as someone doesn't like the way they look and wants to look better so they Photoshop their picture, or as deceptive as portraying a completely different life online than they do in real life. It can be dangerous, though, if someone lies about who they are to get you to meet them and/or has bad intentions. You do have the potential to be physically hurt. (However, it is important to note that this danger doesn't apply exclusively to people you meet online. There are dishonest folks everywhere, so please, please, please be careful, follow your gut, and do your research!)

A Story

I started dating online after I graduated from college, moved to a different city, and broke off my long-term relationship. I worked from home, and most of my friends lived far away. It was difficult for me to meet new people, and so I went online. I started a few different dating profiles; one on a paid site that attempted to match you with other people, and two others that were free and I could just browse other profiles. I learned a lot in my yearlong stint online, and I was catfished a few times. One person told me he was thirty when he was really forty-five. Another didn't tell me he was married. Most never looked anything like the pictures they posted. Sometimes I would go on a few dates and then it would simply fizzle out.

Then I met an engineer online named David. He messaged me around Christmas, and so I didn't get back to him for a few weeks. When I finally did, we struck up a fun conversation and messaged every day for weeks. Then we decided to meet and swapped phone numbers. He took me on the best first date I've ever been on, and the second date I cooked for him—something I had never done for a guy before. A little over a year later we were engaged.

That's right—I met my husband online! We grew up twenty minutes away from each other, our parents had mutual friends, and we even worked in the same building in the same city, but we met online. It was a fantastic way for us to meet with no pressure, and we really got to know each other before we finally met in person.

Tips for Successful Online Dating

- Always post pictures of yourself in good light. Your profile picture should be of just yourself so there is no confusion as to who you are when people meet you in person after meeting you online. Your profile picture should also look good small, as that is how most people will see it before clicking through to your profile. Then post one with you doing something fun that interests you; for example, an outdoor activity or hobby. Another picture should be you in a group of people to show you are fun and have friends. Post more than just your face; try to have a few long shots of your whole body. If you don't post more than your face, you will lose some people because they will think you are self-conscious.

- There is a cheat for profile pictures, especially if you want more views to your profile. Post a picture that is hard to see you when the image is small. When I did this I used a darker picture, and it was hard to see when the image was small, but when you clicked through it was easy to see it in the larger version. I received a lot more profile visits, and so the site boosted my profile for free and I received much more interest.

Tip: I really tested these ideas during the year I was online. The sites want high activity, so the more you add to your profile the more they will advertise you to potential dates.

- Fill out your profile. Make sure you answer any question the site gives you to appear forthcoming, but keep it concise and easy to read. Rambling will lose people. Generally people are looking for something in another person, and you never know what part of you might pique someone's interest. If you are honest and they don't like things you write, that means they wouldn't like you, so there's no worry in impressing them.

- Be responsive. Always answer the other person. I would advise against being too eager and responding right away, but try to answer within a day or two to keep from losing their interest all together. You never know how many people your interest is talking to, so you want to keep their attention. The other side of this coin is that many times these sites will track how often you respond and might send more people your way because your frequent responses might keep them on the site. Be careful, too, as some sites will show the other person when you read their message, so they may see that you read their message but took a day or two to respond. Your lack of a message could send the wrong message!

- Don't give any personal information. Use only your first name, and never give out your email, address, phone number, company, or last name until you feel you really can trust the person. Never put any of this information on your profiles, and wait until you feel comfortable. These sites all have messaging systems for a reason—to keep you safe. So use them!

- Be honest. Use your real picture and answer questions honestly. If you don't feel comfortable sharing, tell them so. The more honest you are, the better foundation you are building, and the better chance you have at actually continuing a relationship. If you lie, it will be hard for the other person to trust you on other items, even if you only lied about one thing.

- Google them. Once you find out enough information, stalk to be safe. Use their name, occupation, city they live in, or any other helpful information to see if you can find them and make sure they really are who they say they are. This is especially true if you plan to meet them in person. That is a completely safe time to ask for more information so that you can be sure you are meeting the person you think you are.

- Always meet in public places. When you do decide to meet, do so in a public location. Drive yourself and plan something short so you can get away, if need be.

Be Safe

Overall, when meeting new people and starting new relationships, always be safe. If you get that odd gut feeling, trust it. Never put yourself in harm's way, and only pursue relationships with people you feel you can trust.

You are entering a new phase of your life, and so most, if not all, of your relationships will change. By reading this chapter, however, you should now know what to expect and how to navigate all your relationships successfully. We believe in you!

CHEAT SHEET

- Grown-up life is different
  - More "you" time
  - More sleep
  - You're the rookie
  - You're judged as a grown-up
  - Stress about money
  - Coping with these changes

- Family
  - Listen, follow your gut, and learn
  - Mutual respect
  - Acknowledge and thank your parents for everything

- o Treat them how you want to be treated
- o Discuss your problems
- o Apologize
- o Be helpful
- o Say "I love you"
- o Include your parents in your life
- o Graduating from the kids' table
- o Accepting or dodging tough questions
- o Verbal sleight of hand
- o Tell them what they want to hear
- o Disarm the questioner with humor
- o Enjoy the new family dynamic

- Friends
  - o If you're far away
  - o If you're close
  - o Making new friends
  - o Join a professional organization
  - o Join a sports league
  - o Volunteer
  - o Go to church
  - o Take classes that interest you
  - o Use websites to meet people with similar interests
  - o When one of you makes more money

- Love
  - o Continuing your relationship
  - o Long-distance relationships
  - o Be upfront
  - o Be faithful
  - o Be realistic
  - o Ending your relationship
  - o Meeting new people (love)
  - o Office romances
  - o Going out
  - o Online dating
  - o Tips for successful online dating
  - o Be safe

MANAGING THE WORKPLACE
Tori

You're no longer a student! Which means you probably have one desk, or workspace, that you use every day. You'll also generally work in the same building(s) and see the same people almost every day. A big step in becoming a full-time adult is learning how to manage your workplace. We use the term *manage* loosely, of course, but we want to help you control what you can control, which is you. You can't tell others around you what to do, nor can you always control what happens around you, but you can dictate how you react and deal with different situations.

One of my favorite sayings that I learned while vacationing in Hawaii is: "It is what it is, but it can be what you make it." In other words, you can't change what's handed to you, but you can change your entire situation based on how you react.

A Story from Betsy

On your first job, be prepared for anything, and know that whatever your current workspace looks like, it will probably change. When I started my first "grown-up" job (and this is going to sound crazy to you), I shared two computers with the managing partners and one of the part-time account supervisors. And we had email but email was so new that for the most part all we did was email each other. Our clients and most media folks didn't have email yet. After a while, of course, we all had our own computers and email was a standard way of communicating. The firm then bought a building and moved to a different part of town. I was first downstairs in that building and then I was upstairs. I had several different supervisors in the two years I worked in that city for the firm. And then I moved to Arizona for a while, worked for them remotely, and I still continue my relationship with many of those same (amazing) people today (thank you, Facebook!)—twenty-two years later! Bottom line: embrace where you are and don't worry if things aren't perfect—they will change shortly regardless!

What Is Different?

First, let's think about what is different in your daily life that might lead to a transition or change in behavior.

No Teachers

For the first time in your life, you don't have a teacher or professor giving you assignments. You no longer have that constant encourager (or discourager) who knows you and can change the outcome of your academic career.

No Grades

You no longer get graded on each piece of work. You can't disregard assignments or pieces of work because you can do well on another project and get an "A" anyway. In fact, the opposite can be true; disregarding a project may result in you losing your job, which leaves no chance to make up for it later!

No Breaks

You no longer have summers off or winter and spring breaks to "get away" and take a vacation from your work. You can schedule vacations in the full-time adult world, but your job is still there and you need to prep for your vacations, as well as make up for what you missed while you were gone.

No Start-Overs and No Set Road Map

There is no longer an end date to your working situation. In the past you knew that at the end of a semester or year, you would be done with that teacher and those people in your class. You then got a "fresh start" with new people, with no hard feelings because you had to leave to move on. Now, you don't get a clean break from people you can't stand either; there's no summer break from your boss, and no way to get out of a project with a co-worker you can't stand. You also don't have preset classes and someone assigned to help you (like your adviser) get through your career. You don't have a road map for the next four or forty years, so you need to plan it on your own.

So how do you deal with all these changes? That's what we're here to help you with! Change can always be scary, but the rewards are bountiful and worth it!

Validation and Value

There is a constant struggle in younger generations (particularly millennials) with validation. In other words, we need to know that we are doing a good job, and we need to hear it often to feel as if we are providing value to those around us. This has been attributed to many different things, including kids all getting "we participated" sport trophies, even when their team lost. We tend to think it has much more to do with our social culture.

We have created a "validation vacuum" in which no amount of validation is enough, as folks are constantly seeking it. When you post something online, you measure its importance by how many likes, shares, and comments you get. I know that if I don't get many likes on my photos, I generally delete them, because I don't feel like those are important to my online life and therefore my offline life. And this huge dependence on others to make us feel important carries over into the workspace as well. There doesn't appear to be an "enough" feature in all of this—hence the term *validation vacuum*.

While in school you have teachers or professors who give you a grade to validate the work you put into a project. At your job, however, you will be very lucky to find a boss and people to work with who will give you that same amount of validation. Generally you are expected to turn in your work, and your thanks is your paycheck. Often, the only feedback you'll get from higher-ups is in response to something negative that happened, which could even be out of your control. It can be difficult to accept this change, especially for the younger generation who struggles with validation or feeling valued and needs to constantly be provided with a real or metaphoric "stamp of approval."

But please don't feel like you are alone! Not only does your entire generation suffer from the validation vacuum, but other generations have struggled with feeling valued simply based on their title or amount of money they make.

The issue lies in that as a culture, we tend to measure our value by what we do. Unfortunately, as a new graduate, your perceived value may be quite low, and probably will for some time. You see other young graduates succeeding and making money, and you want that for yourself and wonder how and why they may seem better than you. Even in a job you love, this can be a difficult subject. For example, you may love to paint and decorate, but others might judge you as not being "successful" if you work at a paint store. You also probably wouldn't make as much as you potentially could to start out, but it's what you love! And this job may also lead you to where you eventually want to end, which is an important step to take in your career.

A Story

One of my very best friends, Kim, went to college with me and studied marketing. She really wanted to go through an interior design program, but her parents encouraged her to study design consecutively with what they felt would be a more functional degree. Kim graduated and landed a job with an insurance company, which she hated. She didn't like anything about this career except for the fact that it helped her buy a house. After she bought her house (on her own, by the way—a major accomplishment!), she decided she couldn't take it anymore. Kim decided to shift careers and got a job at a paint store. While this move may not make sense to you, she made it with an end goal in mind. While she took a pretty large pay cut, she was able to enter a management training program that would allow her to travel and eventually manage a store and help people design their homes. She's continuing to work on finding value in what she does and the happiness she gets from it.

The point is to find value in what you *do*, not the money you make from it or a title that makes you feel important. Find value internally rather than from external factors to find true happiness in what you do. This hits close to home for me, as it's something I struggle with even while writing this book.

A Story

I have always been a bit overachieving, looking for the next big thing to boost my career and keep my momentum going. When I graduated from college I started writing my first book, and I was a published author by age twenty-five. Other people my age tell me I'm so successful and can't believe I've accomplished as much as I have. But I really struggle internally with my career choices. Because I'm always looking to develop new parts of my career as an author and speaker, and I also love to coach cheerleading, it's difficult for me to have a full-time job (besides the fact that I hate working in an office 9-to-5 and completely disagree with the entire premise of it).

Because of this, while I have some very fun and exciting projects, jobs, and accomplishments under my belt, I really make close to nothing. I work extremely long hours on generally three jobs at a time, hoping that my time put in with startups and writing/speaking will pay off in the end. I've been known to go from 7 a.m. until 1 a.m., only stopping for quick bites to eat and to stand up and stretch my legs. But I make less than half of what my husband makes, and much less than most of my friends. Does this mean I'm not successful? No. Does it make me feel like I'm not successful? Definitely. It's hard to feel valuable when you aren't making many dollars!

A Story from Betsy

Don't always follow the money. When I graduated from college, I had two job offers—one was an entry-level job in my field and one as an executive assistant for a company I worked for during college. The executive assistant job offer was close to 50 percent more than the entry-level job in my field. Back then that was a lot of money, and even now that's a big difference. I talked to my dad, who told me to take the job I would enjoy the most and that would start me on the path toward where I wanted to go. So I took the lower-paying job, and I struggled to pay rent for a while, but I quickly moved up in salary and haven't been sorry for one minute. I never told my friends what I was making starting out for fear that I might not be perceived as successful. This is amusing to me now, of course, and it is a lesson I share with my students.

The takeaway I've learned, and what I continue to remind myself every day, is that your value doesn't come from external measures. Your value comes from doing what you love to do. If you enjoy what you do, and you can benefit or help other people and make a living doing it, then you're worth your weight in gold. Not everyone has the luxury of loving what they do, so you have to love it more for them and realize the value of getting to do what you love.

Motivation

Motivation is all about your work ethic. Working hard and wanting to work make it much easier to stay motivated. Sometimes, though, finding ways to stay motivated can be difficult without grades and an end goal (graduation) in sight. Extra credit doesn't exist anymore, and so you have to do your own work. You also have to do your best work every time. If you catch yourself simply thinking that all you have to do is show up to work every day, stop it! The more you think that way, the more you will get sick and tired of your daily routine. Here are a few things you can do to keep yourself motivated on a daily basis:

Know Why You're Working

Have a clear view of what you are working on and what you are accomplishing, exactly, and who it impacts. Once you define that purpose and subsequent goals, you will know when you are successful. If you don't have a clear view of what you are doing, how will you know when you've done it?

Prioritize Your Workload

Once you know exactly what you're doing, make sure you know what is most important. When you finish the higher-importance items first, you automatically make your work more valuable, and that makes you feel better about what you've finished. You can also try to work on different types of projects when prioritizing so that you can break up the same types of work. In other words, try not to do the same thing for eight hours. Divide a writing project over a couple of days, or a busy-work project that will take a lot of time. That way you don't feel as if you've been doing the same thing all day. Break it up with smaller, easier-to-complete items so you feel accomplished.

Celebrate Wins

Even the little ones! Once you've finished every project, celebrate yourself. Buy yourself your favorite treat, go out after work with your friends, or have a glass of champagne (depending on your company culture, you'll probably have to wait until you get home to do so!). Understand when you've accomplished something you should be proud of, and reward yourself for it.

Take Time for Yourself

Take five to ten minutes every hour for yourself. Everyone needs a break sometimes. Especially in our new work culture in which computers and screens have a tight hold on your eyeballs for eight hours or longer per day, it is important to take small breaks. Get up, stretch, walk to get water, focus your eyes on something besides a computer screen, and take a few deep breaths. It will refresh your mind and body and set you up for the next hour of work.

Make Use of Your Skills

Talk to your boss about your skills, and what projects (or types of projects) make you feel like you are really contributing. Focus on showcasing your best skills in your work to keep yourself motivated.

Clean Your Workspace

Getting a new perspective on your workspace can work wonders. Reorganize your space and clean it out. Try not to clutter your workspace, and only put things out that you need access to or will make you smile. Pictures

Organize Your Physical Space

Your office space has an impact on what other people think of you. If you keep your space messy, they may think you aren't responsible, and if someone comes up and asks you for an update on a project and it takes you ten minutes just to search through your own pile of papers, you'll only be proving them right. Therefore, keep your desk or workspace organized and clean. This does not mean that you throw every piece of paper that comes into your office space in a random drawer. This would make your space neat, but not organized. It means setting up a system that makes sense to you, so you know where to find items for projects you are currently working on, past items, and upcoming projects that you know will happen in the future (or recurring projects).

A Story

I have never been a very organized person. I like to think it's because creative people tend to not be very organized. If someone can implement an organization system for me, I am fairly good at following it—until something enters my space and I'm not sure where it goes or how to add it to the already implemented system. My mom and sister are (quite the opposite) fantastic organizers, to the point of labeling clear storage containers for shoes, clothes, and extra items they don't use daily. When I bought my house with my husband, all of the kitchen items stayed in boxes for weeks, because the mere thought of trying to figure out where everything was supposed to go gave me nightmares. My mom and sister came over to help me figure out that the pans should go under the stove, the glasses over the dishwasher, and the silverware under the plates. Now I can keep it organized, but it took a while to get me there.

So I've done some "research" with my loved ones (mostly with those most organized around me), and the following are some steps to keep you from creating piles everywhere and then shoving piles into drawers to get them out of the way.

Start Fresh

Remove everything from your desk and go through it. If you haven't had to look at something in over a year, it's probably OK to throw it away. If that makes you uneasy, consider creating a place to put very old documents that won't take up space that you may need for daily items.

Tip: My friend, Anne, is in graduate school and advises that if you think you might continue your education, you should save notes, tests, and papers to study for graduate placement exams, or even to use if you end up teaching later. I also save many of my old college textbooks and notes for my professional life in case I have a question that can be answered by work I've already completed. Why make more work for yourself, right?

Prioritize Your Items

Decide what you need access to every day versus once per week versus once per month versus only once per year or less. You'll probably always need pens and pencils, so those should be in a drawer that is easy to get to. You probably won't need access to your employee handbook as often, so that can go in a low drawer, high shelf, or behind other items that you will need more often.

Give the Top of Your Desk High Real Estate

Consider the top of your desk as priority real estate. In other words, if your office was a city, the top of the desk would be the most expensive place to live, and so only a few items that are most important should live there. This will probably include your computer, a cup of pens, a clock, or something you need very often that you like having on your desk. Always have less items than you think you need out, because that will keep your desk from looking cluttered when you need to pull work out and spread it out on your desk.

Get Folders for Loose Papers

You will most likely always have loose papers, and it doesn't always make sense to paperclip or staple them. Always have a few folders available to throw loose pages in to keep your desk looking clean and organized. This folder can also be put into a drawer and easily pulled back out if you need to run from your desk and don't want to leave it out.

Develop a Filing System

When you've pulled everything out of your desk, it is a good time to go through your papers and find an easy way to organize them. Label your folders so you can find everything easily, and put them in order of priority.

Organize Your Cords

It's easy for your computer cord, lighting cords, and chargers to get messy very quickly. Try using little twist ties (which you can easily pick up from the grocery store) to tie your cords together so you don't have to worry about them getting tangled or looking like you haphazardly threw wire everywhere.

Find a Place for Your Purse and Pocket Items

You'll always bring a phone, keys, purse, wallet, and other items into your office space. Dedicate an out-of-sight place to put these items for both cleanliness and security. You don't want someone walking by while you're in the restroom to see your phone and pick it up. Keeping it out of sight will ensure your items are safe, and you'll be able to be more focused not waiting for it to light up or ring.

Most important in keeping your workspace clean and organized is to dedicate a little bit of time every day to keep it organized. Organize as you go! I recommend that you schedule time at the same time of day every day to organize your desk. There are two times I don't recommend, however; when you first get to work and right before you leave. Sometimes you will have a lot of work (emails, questions, requests, etc.) come to you the moment you get to work in the morning, and you will prioritize the work over your organization. At the end of the day you might be simply too tired to tackle the organization and go home without setting yourself up for success the next day. Try to set up a habit in which every day around lunchtime, or midmorning/midafternoon break, you take a look at your desk or office space and make any adjustments to your organization system. Clean off the top of your desk (always good to have some cleansing wipes around for times like this), throw away some trash from your snack, or de-clutter your desk surface.

Note from Betsy: Plus, an organized desk and work area just looks good! Think of the folks you know who have clean desks and clean offices. You probably really think highly of them, and think that they have their act together. Don't you want people to think that about you?

When your space is clean and organized, you'll feel clean and organized. It will be much easier for you to keep yourself motivated and working hard on all of your projects.

Manage Interruptions (and Stay Focused!)

There are so many things that can interrupt us during the day and get us off track and challenge our time management plans. For a day or two, jot down some notes as to what some of these things are for you. We are certain that you will start to see patterns, and this is when you can really make progress. Everyone has a few categories of things that frequently interrupt them, and knowledge of what they are is the first step toward managing these time-suckers.

Phone Calls

Perhaps you find that your phone is constantly ringing and causing interruptions. Think about how to best deal with this. Perhaps for an hour or two each day you could let the phone go to voicemail, and then you can return calls all at once to save time and keep your energy focused. Perhaps you can change the wording of your voicemail to encourage people to email you instead, or that you return calls every day during a certain time period so they'll know when you will call them back. Also, leave a number to call for emergencies if there truly is one.

Office Visitors

Many of us are interrupted by office visitors—folks stopping by for work-related or other reasons—and sometimes they are stopping by for "good" reasons, but even if that's the case, usually what they want to talk to you about is not both important AND urgent. These are really the only good reasons for interrupting someone when they are working. If you have a door, perhaps you can have a few hours a day when it is shut, and you put a sign up that says, "Please only knock if your message is both important and urgent. If not, please email me and I'll get back to you later."

If you don't have a door, you can still let your colleagues know that certain times are "office hours" and that you really would like them to respect those time frames and leave you alone. Another way to "shut the door" metaphorically is to spend some time not answering emails and texts, as mentioned above, so you are working on your daily priorities and not others'.

A Story

My mom used to "spoil herself" by grabbing breakfast and her laptop and crawling back into bed when my dad left for work to ease into her day and check her email. But then she found that she was sometimes still in bed answering email at noon or 1 p.m., as the parents of the cheerleaders she coached would barrage her when they knew she was available to answer email. This only gave her an hour or so to prepare for class and nothing on her to-do list checked off. Now, she gets up, gets dressed and ready for the day, and checks her own to-do list before looking at her email.

If people still come in, try to shorten the conversation by saying something like, "I am on a deadline, can I talk to you about this in an hour (or whatever time period is appropriate)?" We are sure you will think of some great ideas as well that will work at your workplace. Smiling, not frowning or growling, when you deliver these messages will go a long way toward training people to respect your uninterrupted time. And this probably goes without saying—please respect others' uninterrupted time as well.

Instant Messaging

Here is one of the few areas where we disagree, so we thought it would be fun to share both of our perspectives, and hopefully one will be helpful to you.

Betsy: I hate instant messaging. I find it insanely annoying and intrusive (and did I mention annoying?), and I turn it off on everything. I've never been tempted to use it, and in fact I get upset if I forget to turn it off and someone IM's me; therefore, I have just eliminated it from my life. As a result, I do not have this type of interruption.

Tori: I LOVE instant messaging. I use it frequently, especially because I work virtually with just about all of my clients. Professionally, I use it to get quick answers to questions or encourage someone to answer an email. Personally I use it to connect with people for urgent or important reasons. I also instant message people to let them know if I am on a conference call or am unable to respond at the moment.

You really need to weigh your options and decide if the good out-weighs the bad with instant messaging. If it can help you get your work done more quickly and the occasional interruption is worth it, go for it! If your network and friends use it to distract you too often and you can't get the work done as quickly, turn it off.

Tip: Set yourself as "away" online. It isn't a big issue for friends, family, and co-workers to just want to say "hi" or ask a quick question, but if it happens constantly throughout the day it can be difficult for you to get anything done. Set yourself as "busy," "away," or even "offline" so that you can get your work done and chat later.

Create Your White Noise

Some people work best with music playing in the background, while others prefer complete silence. Some people, including me, need a lot of chaos around them so they can shut everything out (I can't listen to music because I end up choreographing dances or routines to the tune). Find what you work best to, and then use headphones to get you there. Either put headphones in and play music or use them as glorified earplugs. I've been known to put on a series on Netflix and play it in the background through my earphones because the talking helps me feel as if I can shut everything out. (Note from Betsy: If I'm working from home, I love to find a sporting event [everything except for golf—that's TOO relaxing to listen to!] and have it on in the background. The murmur keeps me company and focused.)

Emails

Don't check personal emails in the morning. Personal emails can side-track you, and without knowing it you can waste a lot of precious time on reading through emails that aren't important to your daily tasks. Set aside time to check your personal emails at lunch or after work.

Set up email filters. A way to help keep yourself from checking your personal emails, or getting sucked into your favorite e-newsletters or spam, is to set up filters. Use filters so that you only receive the most important, high-priority items. Of course, make sure you check your filters every few hours in case something happened to get stuck that was supposed to get through, but this will definitely help to keep you on task.

Social Media

Limit time on social media. It really goes without saying. It's extremely easy to get caught scrolling through your Facebook feed, liking Instagram photos, reading your favorite Tumblr posts, or watching every related video on YouTube. Limit yourself on how much social media you use per day so that you can still get your work done. Some companies may have policies on social media use as well, so make sure you know the rules prior to visiting sites. Many companies will track computer usage, so this can be dangerous to your position and potential career.

Internet Browsing

A fantastic way to keep yourself off social media and stay focused on your computer tasks is to close all programs and browser tabs that you aren't using. If I leave a tab open on my browser to check back on later and I notice it while working the next day, it is much too easy to get lost back in that side project or follow-up item that I left open. Closing the possibilities will keep you accountable and on task.

Make Yourself Comfortable

It's a lot easier to work when you're happy, and an easy way to keep yourself happy is to keep yourself comfortable. Get yourself a comfortable office chair and set it at an appropriate height for good posture. I like to sit on an exercise ball while I work (not only is it better for me, but I get to roll around and move while I work), and some have adopted the standing desk, in which the desk is high enough to stand while working. Any of these options are wonderful, as long as you are happy.

Staying focused will keep you on track to finishing your projects on time, which will keep you happy, stress-free, and ultimately motivated to keep moving forward.

Communication

Everything we've covered so far in managing your workspace has to do with how you function internally and your physical workspace. But there are many more people in your office, and you need to know how to manage your relationships, or lack thereof, with them as well.

Company Culture

Each company has its own culture, or way that it operates, with its own rules and traditions. Some companies have a fun, light-hearted atmosphere where you can wear casual clothing, eat free snacks, and ride your skateboard through the office. Others are much more professional, where you are required to wear business clothing, keep quiet to respect others around you, and keep out of your co-workers' space. (And, sadly, no free snacks.)

Understanding your company's culture is the first step to communicating well with those around you. You can figure out your company's culture by reading the handbook, mission, and other items, or by asking your supervisor. It's best to ask this question early, but if you ever have a question you should feel comfortable asking your boss what is appropriate. Then respect that company culture. This will affect everything you do in the office, from how you dress to how you deal with people of the opposite sex and dating.

Personality Types A, B, C, and D

Once you know the company culture, it's important to know how different types of people like to be dealt with. Everyone is different, but it is generally accepted via the research of numerous psychologists that there are four types of people that you will communicate with. As such, knowledge of these types is needed to understand why these people react the way they do. Suzanne Barston, bizMe writer, wrote recently about how these personality types are important to pay attention to in the workplace. We agree!

To remind you (or share with you for the first time), here is a summary of the four types:

Type A

Type A personalities only care about the bottom line and don't care to be bothered with the details. Type A's are extremely goal-oriented and care only about the solution, which can make them very competitive. Because of this they tend to be in leadership positions, but they can be bossy or impatient at times.

Type B

Type B personalities are "people's people" and care most about acceptance and what others think of them. They tend to be best at building relationships with others, and they thrive on accomplishments and validation. Type B's can be caught socializing too often, but they are generally able to influence others and accept change. They are often found in sales and marketing positions.

Type C

Type C personalities are the detail people. They aren't as competitive as Type A or B, and they care much more about being right. While Type C's are most interested in accuracy and logic, they can tend to be controlling of others. They are found in leadership positions, and they want all the details before making decisions.

Type D

Type D personalities rely on stability and routine. These are the people in the office that don't mind doing the same thing for long periods of time. Type D's are great listeners and team players, but they can let others take advantage of them or their feelings just to keep the peace.

You've probably known people in your life who exactly define each of these personality types. Some people are mixes of a few of these personality types, while others are exact replicas. I like to think of myself as an A/B, and Betsy is primarily an A, with B and C tendencies. I am very goal-oriented and thrive in entrepreneurial leadership positions, but at the same time I thrive on the validation from others and have been known to oversocialize in office situations (oops!). Betsy is very goal-oriented and good at the details, but also prefers it when folks think she's wonderful.

Now that you understand these different personality types, you know what motivates them. If your boss is a Type A, then you probably shouldn't send them a long, three-page email with every step you took to finish a project. They just need the synopsis. If your boss is a Type C, then you should send them that longer email. If your co-worker is a Type D, make sure you really listen to them and ask them how they feel when you work on a project together to verify you are on the same page. And if your co-worker is a Type B, be careful to not get caught in long conversations.

Obviously some of this is generalization, but the idea is to think before you communicate with different types of people. Get the answer you want from those you work with by knowing how to ask the question correctly. This will also help you to get along with everyone in the office and reduce your stress.

How to Deal with Other People

There are a lot of ways that you can set yourself up for success in dealing with other people. If you can create a strong foundation with a person, then you've set yourself up for success when there are bumps in the relationship road, and you'll know you've done everything you could.

Watch How You Communicate

Even more important than what you say is how you say it. Watch your tone and body language so that what you say isn't interpreted the wrong way or makes the other person feel poorly. Misinterpretations happen most often via electronic communication (email, texts, instant message), so be sure to be clear when you are joking or teasing. Otherwise people might think you are just mean. Reread every piece of electronic communication before you send it. And read it out loud.

Underpromise and Overdeliver

This is an often-used adage for a reason—it works! Always promise less than what you think you will be able to do, then when you can do more you look like a hero. It never helps to promise the BEST case scenario, and then come up short. I've even told people sometimes that I will definitely get A, B, and C done, while working hard to make progress on

D. Then when I finish everything, it looks as if I have gone above and beyond for that person and they are extremely happy.

Be Kind

Being nice to other people is always a good idea. Encourage others and lift them up to make them feel better about themselves. Get caught performing random acts of kindness for others and pay it forward, and it will eventually come back around to you. Everyone loves to receive a compliment, and it can only make you more popular with your co-workers. In fact, consider giving a compliment (or two) every day. This will force you to look for the good in others—a wonderful context to live from!

Be Positive

People love happy people! Always be uplifting around others and they will want to be around you more. Don't dwell on the minor aches or annoyances, and instead focus on the good things that are happening in your life. This will make you more positive and influence others around you.

A Story

The best example I have of an always-happy person is my coauthor, Betsy. She is seriously the happiest person I know, all the time. Not only does it make her fun to be around, but it makes me want to be around her more, introduce her to more people I know, and share things with her. I know it's helped her with her network, too, and other people feel the same way. It's part of her brand, or reputation, and others know her for it.

Don't Gossip

Nothing good can ever come from saying bad things about another person. You never know who is listening, or what will be repeated, and so it's a good idea to keep these things to yourself. You probably shouldn't engage in it with other people as well, and you should avoid those in your office who are known for gossiping. It doesn't make you look professional and can actually hurt your professional reputation, as well as hurt those you gossip about.

Note: All of us have probably been "caught" saying something unkind, and if this has happened to you, you know that it's a horrible feeling. If you make it a policy not to gossip or say mean things, you never have to have this feeling again! Also, when you gossip, sometimes it makes others wonder if you talk about them behind their back as well.

Be Aware of Others' Feelings

This is somewhat covered in not gossiping, but goes a step further. Never make a joke at someone's expense or talk someone down to make yourself look better. It goes back to the Golden Rule—treat others how you want to be treated. Hurting someone else is never good for your workplace or career. (In fact, this never works. When you talk bad about others, usually the one who looks bad is you. Conversely, when you shine a light on others' good works, the light shines right back on you!)

A Story from Betsy

My colleague Jan is a master at shining the light on others, and as a result, everyone she works with loves her. She's a favorite co-worker because she isn't afraid to let others get the spotlight. And, as a result, the spotlight is also on her for being a fabulous person to work with.

Keep an Open Mind to Other Viewpoints

It's never a good idea to get into an argument in the workspace. Try to keep an open mind and accept everyone's different opinions. You will come across looking much more mature if you can disagree without being disagreeable or cranky.

Pay No Heed to What Others Say

While you may practice the Golden Rule and not gossip about others, it doesn't mean people will treat you the same way. Sometimes people will say mean things about you either behind your back or to your face. You can't change the fact that they've said it. They probably have insecurities or other reasons to say mean things. What you should do is not take it to heart and be confident of yourself. You know yourself better than they do, so you know that what they say isn't true. Let your actions shine through and prove them wrong.

Don't Worry about Credit or Affirmation

You won't always get it from others. Do your best and know it's your best. Doing it for someone else will only stress you out more and make you rely more on what others think of you. Be secure in your work and abilities, and thrive off the few comments or compliments you do receive.

Be Respectful

Respect those you work with, both personally and their physical space. If you have food items or lotions that may smell, respect your co-workers by either eating or using those items outside, or avoiding them while at work. Respect them personally and show them through your daily actions and words. Ask them how they are and really listen. Take an interest in their lives and show them you care.

Out-of-Office Work Events

When you are at work events outside of the office, remember you are still presenting yourself professionally. Keep the drinking to one or two alcoholic drinks (at most) and pretend you are still in your office. Treat everyone the same way you have and show your co-workers that you are a true professional inside and outside the office.

Relationships

As discussed in chapter 5, the office is a very easy way for you to meet new people, and this will undoubtedly include friends and potential love interests. It is very important (especially in the love arena) to understand rules that your company may have in practice. After that make sure you continue to be professional in your workspace and not let your relationships get in the way of your work.

Friendships

Friends are wonderful to have in the office, and we definitely recommend making several where you work. Once you've developed these friendships, however, it is important to respect your company and keep your friendly conversations to a minimum while at work. Limit them to your lunch break and appropriate water-cooler conversations, and then take the longer conversations out with you after work to the restaurant or your phone conversations.

Love Relationships

Be very cautious here, as feelings can often get in the way of getting your job done. It can be fun to work with your love interest, until you are in a fight, others gossip about you, or you break up. You don't want to let that three-week boyfriend or girlfriend get in the way of your career goals. Some cases are special, but those are the odd cases, and you shouldn't assume that yours will work out. I'll share one of mine that didn't.

A Story

While I was interning for a company, there was one co-worker who was only a few years older than I was. He was a really nice guy, and we became friends almost instantly because we were the youngest in the office and had an unspoken camaraderie. After a few months, we started to hang out after work and spend time with other friends from the office who were close to our age. When I broke up with my boyfriend at the time, he was my shoulder to cry on, and we started to develop a dating relationship.

The dating continued for a few months, but soon it was over. After that, he decided to move and work somewhere else, but it was awkward for others in the office, and one of my co-workers even said to me that I had changed him and she missed the "old him." It was awful all around, and I regretted the decision as we aren't even friends anymore. It didn't make me look good and could have potentially hurt my career if that was my permanent job.

Different Ages

One big difference from college to adult life is the ages of the people you work with. You will undoubtedly work with people of many different ages, and this can be both beneficial and difficult. Where possible, try to show your know-how, but realize that your older co-workers have much more life and work experience than you. We will talk much more about communicating with those older than you, and how to benefit from these relationships, in the next chapter.

CHEAT SHEET

- What is different?
  - No teachers
  - No grades
  - No breaks
  - No start-overs and no set road map

- Validation and value

- Motivation
  - Know why you're working
  - Prioritize your workload
  - Celebrate wins
  - Take time for yourself
  - Make use of your skills
  - Clean your workspace
  - Read, read, read
  - Get feedback

- Organization
  - Organize your time
  - Organize your projects
  - Organize your physical space
  - Start fresh
  - Prioritize your items
  - Give the top of your desk high real estate
  - Get folders for loose papers
  - Develop a filing system
  - Organize your cords
  - Find a place for your purse and pocket items

- Managing interruptions (and stay focused!)
  - Phone calls
  - Office visitors

- o Instant messaging
- o Create your white noise
- o Emails
- o Social media
- o Internet browsing
- o Make yourself comfortable

- Communication
  - o Company culture
  - o Personality types A, B, C, and D

- How to deal with other people
  - o Watch how you communicate
  - o Underpromise and overdeliver
  - o Be kind
  - o Be positive
  - o Don't gossip
  - o Be aware of others' feelings
  - o Keep an open mind to other viewpoints
  - o Pay no heed to what others say
  - o Don't worry about credit or affirmation
  - o Be respectful
  - o Out-of-office work events

- Relationships
  - o Friendships
  - o Love relationships
  - o Different ages

CHAPTER SEVEN
MAINTAINING CAREER MOMENTUM
Tori

So you have your first "career job," and, chances are, you love it! Most college students, upon graduation and finding their first career job, are ecstatic and can be caught in a "honeymoon" stage with their new position. We encourage you to cherish these moments and really throw yourself into your new job. But what happens next? Or what if you don't love your your first job? We've already discussed how life will be different for you now that you aren't a student anymore, but what do you work toward now that you aren't working for a diploma? This chapter will help you keep yourself motivated, make the right decisions, and continue loving (or move toward loving) your chosen career!

A Story

When I first graduated from college I struggled with not feeling as if I was doing enough. I was accustomed to long days of schoolwork, student organization meetings, internships, and more, resulting in a few awards, my college diploma, and a full-time job. It was difficult, however, for me to make the transition to a 9-to-5 job, and I wanted to figure out how I could continue to push myself. I took a day to really work out my LIFE PRIORITIES list (per chapter 1) and discovered that I wanted much more from my career than an office job. I decided a regular job just wasn't for me. On my LIFE PRIORITIES list, I discovered that something I really wanted to do was write a book. I decided that this could really help me prove

151

that I was a thought leader on a subject, and it would be a much more interesting and impressive business card to give to people.

When I looked at the seasons of my life, I realized that there was no better time than the present to write a book because I was single, working, and living on my own. I felt the need to continue the momentum I'd built up in school for myself. Three years later my first book with Betsy was published, and that momentum has continued into this book as well. Just as Betsy discussed in chapter 1, though, I didn't stop there. I looked at my LIFE PRIORITIES list after our first book came out and decided what else I wanted to do. I decided that becoming a speaker on the topics of our books, as well as starting my own business, were important pieces to my overall career. A year later, I was speaking at the Central California Women's Conference and was able to launch my own company, Brand Chicks, with Betsy and a few other amazing women.

The point is to never get lazy or give up on your career. Just as when you were a student, you should always be fighting to better yourself and your career situation. Always set your next goal, evaluate your work toward that goal, establish a new goal, and so on. We'll cover a few specific ways that you can work your way toward your motivated, winning career.

Be Indispensable

The best way to solidify your career and make sure you are always in control is to make yourself indispensable to your supervisor and to your whole organization. This means that you want to make it nearly impossible for anyone to let you go, because what would they ever do without you?

Do Your Supervisor's Thinking for Them

The best thing you can do is make your boss's job easier. Not only should you only ever give them your best work (remember, you aren't graded anymore, so you have to be the final say regarding the quality of all of your own projects), but when possible you should strive to think ahead as well. If you know that an important meeting is coming up, ask what you can prepare ahead of time to help your boss with that meeting. Don't wait to be asked to put together things that come up on a regular basis. You know you need to do it, so do it BEFORE you are asked. Anticipate. Use initiative.

Note from Betsy: Nothing is better than going into a meeting with an intern or student and having the conversation turn to something I would like them to do and having it already done because they were anticipating the need. Or, better yet, having them provide me with information that I hadn't even thought of yet.

Champion Your Boss

A great way to help yourself is to talk-up your boss. If more people think your boss is great and your boss loves you, people will trust your boss's seal of approval of you. This doesn't mean you have to be the "teacher's pet" of the job world, but it does mean you should always speak well of your boss. This can only help you, and when your boss hears about what you've been saying, they'll be happier, too. Be authentic, of course, and champion the parts of your boss that you truly admire or treasure. The other parts—don't discuss in public. And we hope this goes without saying, but never post anything negative about your job EVER on social media. This does nothing to build your brand, and it can only harm it or perhaps even get you fired. If you are really upset about something at work, talk to your significant other or parent or best friend. Vent, adjust, do whatever you need to do, but keep it offline.

Help Your Boss Achieve Goals

We talked briefly about working toward your company's goals in chapter 6, and now you'll want to help your boss achieve his or her goals as well. This will be very noticeable to your boss and make him or her want to keep you on as long as possible because you help them! Step one here is to make sure you understand your boss's goals—so ask your boss what they are! Do they want increased sales? New clients? Find out what your boss's personal goals for your department or company are, and then you can help to achieve those.

Note: While doing all of these things for your boss, you may be discouraged if he/she doesn't seem to appreciate you or your efforts. Please do not get upset! You can't get along with everyone, and unfortunately this can occasionally apply to your boss. You also can't assume that your boss knows how valuable you truly are, and how much they would miss you if you weren't there. Keep with it and do your best!

Be the Go-To Person to Get Things Done

How do you do this? Get things done! Sounds easy, right? But this means even finding ways to get difficult things done. Also, don't make excuses. Just get it done. Figure it out. You want people to come to you when there is a problem because you are always able to figure it out. Find a way to get everything done, make connections in other departments, and keep Google search at the ready in case it's as simple as an Internet search!

Become an Expert in Your Niche/Skill Set

No one knows everything about everything, but if you can know everything (or at least most things) about your specific niche or skill set, you can propel your career in the right direction! The people you work with will recognize your knowledge, and you'll prove that you are important to your department or company.

Be a PS, Not a PI

We both fully believe in this idea, so let me explain. We want you to be a problem SOLVER, not a problem IDENTIFIER. In other words, if you notice that the paper is out in the printer, replace the paper—don't simply tell everyone it's out of paper. If you notice that there is something wrong with a project or idea, work to fix it before you blurt out that something is wrong. Learn to take the extra moment to think through the problem to see if you can come up with a solution. This will prove that you are not only observant but also know how to fix issues.

We've all worked with (or at least known) people who are problem identifiers. They are usually negative, or just like to point out when things are going wrong, but they hardly ever have a solution or anything good to say about it. We don't want you to be one of these people, because people don't like to spend time with problem identifiers.

Also, being a problem identifier is easy—anyone can do that! It takes skill and creative thinking to be a problem solver, so that's the path that we highly recommend.

Be a Team Player

Go the extra mile for others in your organization. If people know you will go to bat for them, or know that you care about the team more than (or at least as much as) yourself, they will be more willing to come to you when they are in need, and that's exactly when you can shine and help them out. We've probably all heard the old saying, "There's no 'I' in 'team.'" This is true outside of team sports, and you should keep this in mind on group projects or department events. Never take full credit for anything, and instead build up your team. If people catch you taking credit for everything, they might be less willing to bring you projects in the future, especially if they want some credit for themselves, too.

Be Taken Seriously

Another important step to being successful in your current position is finding how to be taken seriously. As a student, you were probably used to people asking you a lot of questions about your dreams and goals, but as a full-time adult you may be surprised to find how little those questions will be asked now. After you graduate from college, adults will rarely ask you what your career goals are after you have your first position. I find this very odd, because you should always have your next goal in mind, always be working toward it, and be telling everyone around you so they can help you make it happen. To be taken seriously, though, it's time to get focused on your more immediate future.

Focus on Your Current Projects

It can be tempting to daydream about your career goals or even work on your LIFE PRIORITIES list at work, but this is a surefire way to prove to others around you that you don't take your current job seriously. When you're at work, make sure you are in your work frame of mind and fully committed to your projects. This will not only prove that you are completely engrossed in what you need to be doing but also show your dedication to the company.

A Story

I generally will schedule most of my tweets during the weekdays so that I don't have to stop during my workday to look up articles. I want to be sure that when I'm in work mode, I'm fully in work mode. This became a problem once when my boss at the time thought that I was tweeting those in real time. He got upset and told me it made it look as if I wasn't fully committed to the job during the day. I told him that I scheduled them out a week in advance, but he still wasn't very happy. I could have handled it better by telling him up front, but I honestly didn't think much of it. In the future, I will of course be more up front about it, and hopefully you can learn from my experience as well (more on social media a little later in this chapter!).

Act Mature

A great way to be taken seriously is to act mature. Gone are the days when you could act like a college student while an intern for a company. Hopefully you are mature and won't need to "act it," but the idea is to focus on acting like the full-time adult you are now. You want to act for the job you want in the future, not the job you have right now. Pay attention to those around you and who you think acts appropriately, or who is well received by others. Odds are that you will probably want to act like them. Start to attempt to mimic their actions and words, and see if it affects the way others treat you in the workplace.

Respect Your Elders

It's really easy as a twenty-something to think we know everything (believe me, I know!), but we don't. This is a good time for you to look at your accomplishments and goals and measure them with others in your office and what they have accomplished. Chances are people you work with have done some pretty amazing things, and you can use this limited opportunity to learn as much as you can from them. Betsy will talk much more about this in chapter 8, Mentors and Mentoring, but the idea is to respect those older than you and always assume they know more than you do. Every once in a while you might be surprised to find that they will ask for your advice on something, but never go in assuming and giving out advice without them asking for it.

A Story

When I started at a new company once, I was brought in to do some social media work with another woman. She was older than I was, with three daughters and a lot of life experience. When I walked in I was completely happy to step back and listen to her, taking in everything they were doing in social media and seeing how I could help. I knew a lot about social media, and I had an opinion on pretty much everything she said, but I kept them completely to myself. Once she felt comfortable with me, she started asking me questions, and I was happy to share my opinions and expertise. Within a few weeks we learned that her gift was really client relations, and mine was the social media strategy. We built up a lot of trust asking each other for help and have maintained a solid friendship since that point.

Dress for the Job You Want

A very important way to be taken seriously at work is to look serious. And so you should dress for the job you want, not the job you have right now. If you want to be a CEO, you probably should wear suits all the time. If you are more of an artsy person, you can probably get away with a more casual look. If you want a job in fashion, you should probably invest in some interesting fashion pieces to impress those in your industry. This is another opportunity for you to observe those around you and see who impresses you with their dress to help you decide on your own clothing choices.

A Story

A very recent, fun story between Betsy and I was when I went to speak at the Central California Women's Conference. There was a speakers' dinner the night before, and because Betsy helps to put the conference on, we were both invited. It was 100 degrees (or hotter) outside, and I wasn't accustomed to the hot weather. I had only brought slacks and a button-down blouse, which sounded like no fun in the heat. I text messaged Betsy to ask her if she thought it would be appropriate for me to wear capris with the button-down blouse, because I value her opinion on my brand and what other people will probably think of me. She advised me against it by bluntly saying, "You don't want to be confused with the interns." It was funny and we laughed, but of course she was 100 percent right. When I arrived at the dinner I was much closer in age to the interns, and it was more appropriate for me to be dressed more formally than they were for the occasion. Plus, they wanted me to get up and give a mini commercial of my speaking topics, and so I felt more comfortable in front of them.

A Story from Betsy

As faculty, we don't have a dress code, and many of my colleagues across campus dress very informally. When I began to teach, I first thought this was pretty cool, and I considered wearing casual clothes. But then I thought about my brand, and I decided that if I were teaching public relations and wanted my students to end up as practicing and successful public relations professionals, I needed to dress like a public relations professional. As a result, I dress differently than some of my colleagues, but I don't mind, because I'm staying true to my brand.

Follow Up

Following up on all items is very important to help others take you seriously. Confirm all meetings, email everyone back (in a timely manner), and make sure others feel as if you've come full circle. You'll come across as dependable and very serious about your choices. Plus, if you follow up on everything, you'll save yourself time later trying to remember if someone ever emailed you back. Just keep notes for yourself so you know who was taking the next step on each of your projects.

Solidify Your Brand

We've talked a bit about your brand, or reputation, already, but it bears repeating! Your professional brand is essential to your career momentum, and your brand could either build your career or kill it. There are many ways to build your brand, and I'll cover some of our favorites.

Punctuality

This is very important to your brand, and it is often an overlooked piece of etiquette. If you show up late often, it will be hard to prove to others through your actions that you really care about them or what you are working on. It only makes you look as if you don't have everything together because you can't get yourself there on time. Not only can it be annoying to others, but they may feel as if you are wasting their time. Betsy recommends that you strive to be four minutes early to everything. I always give myself fifteen minutes, mostly because I don't trust myself, the traffic in the San Francisco Bay Area, or anything else that can go wrong. I figure that fifteen minutes can save me if I can't find the location (read: get lost—which happens to me often, even with a GPS!), if I need to grab some gas quickly, or want to run to the bathroom quickly beforehand. Find whatever works for you and stick with it. It will be much better for you to be early and have some solid prep/thinking time before your meeting than to run in late and feel flustered and stressed.

Have Good Vocabulary

Another often overlooked quality is having good vocabulary. You can impress others with your knowledge and only improve your brand. Don't use big words just to use big words, but stretch yourself a bit to learn new words and try them out. You might even find it fun!

Speak Concisely

Think before you speak. Sounds easy, right? Sometimes it is difficult to really think about what you want to say, and then get it out clearly and concisely. My dad is really good at this, and he is a man of very few words—and a lot of jokes. I know that when I talk to him I have to give him a few seconds to process and then respond, but he will mean everything he says and hardly ever has to put his foot in his mouth. It's something I aspire to, as I often have to go back and stop myself because I love to talk so much! I've learned that if you can put yourself in the right mindset and almost think like you are in the middle of a media interview, often it is easier to speak more concisely, leaving out the small details people really don't need and leaving the conversation open for further discussion. Remember, you always want to leave people wanting more of you!

Connect Others

Betsy is amazing at this, and I hope to be great at this one day as well. You want to find a way to grow your network enough so that you are a connector of people. If someone tells you they need something, hopefully you can use your network to help them find the solution. Not only does this make you look good, it helps both of the people you've connected, and everyone is happy! It's a win-win-win.

Another piece of connecting others is being able to determine what a person's needs really are. It's very rare that a person in your network will come up to you point blank and ask for exactly what they need. You may need to read between the lines and be intuitive to figure out what a potential need for them would be. Then help them solve it. This is very similar to doing the thinking for your supervisor that we talked about earlier, but you want to do it for everyone you know, not just the person who writes your paychecks!

Be a Resource

Being a resource to other people is a fantastic brand-building opportunity. You can share your know-how with others, send articles, or share general trends with others in your network and come across as knowing a lot about your industry and caring about those around you. A great way to do this publicly is via social media, because then you are not only sharing an important piece of information with a network connection but also showing the rest of your network that you are willing to help (and maybe help them, too, if they were looking for that information).

Have People's Backs

Always have other people's backs. We've mentioned this before, but you want to be sure that you steer clear of the gossip and water-cooler talk when your time could be much better used toward building others up and building your brand in the process. Plus, when you lend a co-worker a hand or a friendly gesture, they're much more likely to reciprocate in the future.

Give Compliments

People love receiving compliments! Generally those around you put a lot into what their hair looks like, the clothes they wear, or the accessories they carry. I have never heard of anyone complaining that a person gives too many compliments, and so I really think this is a brand-building opportunity that you can run with. People will remember you for the things you say and will remember how happy you made them feel. And giving compliments not only makes other people happy, but it helps you look for the good in other people as well.

Be Overly Generous with Gratitude

Say thank you, often, about everything. People love to be thanked, and you can only make others feel good about you through your gratitude. Always be willing to give others "shout-outs" and thank them for their hard work. A fantastic way to do this publicly is through social media as well. It shows others that you are grateful for those in your network and gives the person you're thanking some public praise.

There are so many brand-building opportunities, but be careful to ponder each of them and use them. If you don't think about these opportunities, or even neglect some of them, you could potentially hurt your brand by not making some of the positive steps above. For example, if someone does something nice for you and you don't say thank you, they may feel that you are unappreciative, and you don't want that word to be a part of your brand!

Social Media

Arguably the biggest brand-building or killing opportunity is social media. Both Betsy and I are huge advocates of social media for your personal brand, and in fact we went into detail on how to use social media for your career in our first book, *Land Your Dream Career: 11 Steps to Take in College*. We will touch on it here, but if you would like more detail about posting, management, and more, please check out our first book!

Social media has become a part of everyday life, and unfortunately, many people don't really think before posting. As a cheer coach, I see many posts from teenagers that I know they will regret one day but they haven't learned about how wide the Internet really is, yet. It's an issue for all future generations, as many people are growing up online and on social media (either via their own or their parents' social media sites). Lucky for you, you're reading this book! Please be aware that everything you post online is public, no matter what your privacy settings are. There are ways for people to hack, screenshot, share, or steal any information, and so you MUST be careful about everything you post and be sure that your posts build your brand.

That being said, we are both huge advocates of social media and highly recommend it as a brand-building opportunity for every professional.

Integrate into Your Brand

Step one when setting up your social profiles and posting is to be sure that you integrate your brand into your profiles. Make sure you have a professional headshot, use a professional name, and then be consistent on all platforms. You want to be sure that it's obvious to people who find you online that you are really you. Chances are there are other people with your same name out there, and you need to differentiate yourself from them. Add a middle initial if you need to, or even use a nickname. Then make sure your picture is always the same so that people will recognize you and have no question that your network is yours. Consistency is key here, and the more consistent you are, the easier it will be for people to remember you and your brand.

Post Carefully and Strategically

You should only post things that add value to your network. This can include news, trends, fun facts, how-to's, and fun things, but you should pepper in your knowledge whenever possible. Social media gets a bad rap as some people think that users only blast out what they are doing and not providing value. While this is true for many social media users, we hope that you will be the exception. Rather than posting you are eating a sandwich, try to post where you are eating that sandwich, if they have a special promotion, when they are open, or something else to entice others to go there. This will provide value to your following and make that business very happy.

Think First—Does This Post Help or Hurt My Brand?

The most important question to ask yourself before posting anything on social media is whether the specific post will help or hurt your brand. If the answer is anything less than help, don't post it. There is no reason to! You only want to use social media as a brand-building opportunity. Many people respond to this negatively and think we take all the fun out of social media. This is not the case! You can still share pictures of you and your friends at a football game, or your new puppy, but think twice before posting yourself with a red party cup in hand, or when you are out at a bar. Not only will these pictures generally be unattractive, they can make you look cheap and unprofessional. Save those pictures for texting back and forth, and keep them off social media.

A Story

One of my friends was in a sorority in college, and she and her sisters would play "hide the red cup" when they were at a party and knew pictures would end up online. The red Solo™ cup has become a bit of a taboo in online pictures, as they are generally full of alcohol. My friend and her sisters would hide the cups when cameras were pulled out, or when they took pictures of each other. They wanted pictures having fun together, but they didn't want to broadcast the drinking parts of their outings.

Tip: You can set up filters on social media sites such as Facebook so that you have to approve the tagging of pictures before they can show up on your profile. We recommend this so that you don't have random, unhelpful pictures popping up unexpectedly when someone in your professional network is on your profile.

Be a Thought Leader

An important part of maintaining your career momentum is establishing yourself as a thought leader in your industry. Not only will this help you, but your organization and those in your network will see you as a person "in the know" in your industry, which will help your brand. Your goal should be that people on social media will come to you with questions or ask you for help online, for which you can forward them to your organization or even take on some extra work.

When to Stay and When to Go

An integral part of moving forward in your career is knowing when to stay in your current role and when to leave. This is something that a lot of people struggle with, not just young professionals. I'll preface this section with the fact that it is not a good idea to quit your job every time you are unhappy or uncomfortable. When you feel uneasy, you are generally in a new situation, which means you have the opportunity to learn something from the situation. And in fact, every time you have a job you should be learning something. In fact, if you are too comfortable, it might be time for you to move on and find something that challenges you more.

My favorite piece of advice I received so far in my young career was from a recent boss who told me that when I was no longer learning from my job, it was time to move on. Her theory was that your job should be much more than a paycheck to you, and if you're only taking home money and no knowledge, then the company is getting more from you than you are from it. This has helped me a lot in my growing career, as I've made some important life decisions based on the fact that I was or wasn't learning something. Now I strive to always be uncomfortable in what I'm doing, and I know that means I'm pushing myself to a new and better level.

CHEAT SHEET

- Be indispensable
  - Do your supervisor's thinking for them
  - Champion your boss
  - Help your boss achieve goals
  - Be the go-to person to get things done
  - Become an expert in your niche/skill set
  - Be a PS, not a PI
  - Be a team player

- Be taken seriously
  - Focus on your current projects
  - Act mature
  - Respect your elders
  - Dress for the job you want
  - Follow up

- Solidify your brand
  - Punctuality
  - Have good vocabulary
  - Speak concisely
  - Connect others

- Be a resource
- Have people's backs
- Give compliments
- Be overly generous with gratitude

- Social media
  - Integrate into your brand
  - Post carefully and strategically
  - Think first—does this post help or hurt my brand?
  - Be a thought leader

- When to stay and when to go

MENTORS AND MENTORING
Betsy

M entors are fabulous! If you have one, you know this, and if you don't, you probably still know this to be true. Right here and now we'd like to do a big-time "shout-out" to all people who are mentors. On behalf of the world—THANK YOU! We wouldn't be where we are without you!

People talk about mentors a lot, but many people don't know how to get one, what to do with one, and whether or not they need more than one. All of that is covered in this chapter, as well as the importance of you serving as a mentor as well, even at this early stage of your career. You'll learn about the growing trend of reverse mentoring and how young professionals can give back to their mentors and others to further increase their network and influence.

Mentoring is an interesting concept that comes in all shapes, sizes, and directions. Some folks have one lifelong mentor, and some have many different ones for the different stages of their lives. Others have one to help them through a particularly challenging period—and then that's it! You are probably most familiar with traditional mentoring, where an older, more experienced (or "seasoned") person mentors a younger, less experienced person. However, there is also reverse mentoring, a relatively new phenomenon, where a (typically) younger, less experienced person mentors an (typically) older, more experienced one. Reverse mentoring is commonly used with regard to technology, particularly in the area of social media. There is also colleague mentoring, in which people of relatively equal experience mentor each other.

All three types can benefit you greatly. So, of course, we will cover all of them! While there is no "magic" formula for mentoring, there is a lot that has been studied and experienced that can help you make the most out of all of your mentoring adventures.

Note: Before we go any further, we would like to extend a huge thank you to the following amazing mentors and mentees who contributed ideas and wisdom for this chapter: Armen Bacon, Amy Brogan, Jennifer Bulotti, Gregg Champion, Gerard Francis Corbett, Christi Black Davis, Chris Fiorentino, Micheline Golden, Kristie Gonzales, Bonni Montevecchi, Ronald A. Orozco, Candice Pendergrass, Jane Olvera Quebe, Peter Robertson, Darren Rose, Brenda S. Smith, John Wallace, Jill Wagner, Steve Weakland, and Dawn Wilcox.

Why You Need a Mentor

We are guessing that because you are reading this book, we don't have to "sell" you a great deal on why you need a mentor. You are clearly someone who is interested in your overall life success, and you probably intuitively and instinctively know that having someone who "has your back" and can teach you things you don't know is a good thing.

Nonetheless, here are some of the many reasons why having a mentor (or more than one) is good for you and your career:

- Everyone needs a "soft place to fall," meaning a place where you can ask questions, share challenges, and get advice without feeling judged. Good mentors will provide you with a "soft place to fall." I believe I first heard this phrase from Dr. Phil, and I've loved it ever since. I think he was referring to it in a familial context, as in everyone's home should be a "soft place to fall" (which we also agree with 100 percent!), but it applies beautifully to the idea of mentoring as well. Everyone needs this, and your mentor is the perfect person to be this for YOU.

- You need a bigger network. Your network can always benefit from getting bigger, and a good mentor will share his/her network (or parts of it) with you. This is truly priceless (as you know); it is the relationships that you have coupled with your competence that will lead to your ultimate success.

- You'll have problems that you can't solve yourself. Especially as you grow and stretch yourself to take on new skills, projects, and responsibilities, you'll need and want someone to help you solve new problems and challenges.

- A veteran perspective is always helpful, even if you decide to do something contrary to your mentor's advice. Hearing from someone who has "been there" provides you with important context and/or a historical, cultural, and industry context that can help you do what is best for you via looking at the big picture. Even if you choose to go a different direction, having your mentor's perspective will help a great deal.

A Story

One of my favorite mentors (and I am so grateful for all of them!) is my amazing colleague Jan, whom I teach with at Fresno State and also work with on a fabulous event called the Central California Women's Conference. Jan is seventeen years older than I am and a masterful networker, negotiator, and salesperson. I have learned MANY, MANY things by observing her "in action" and through her mentorship. What's funny (and also fun) is that she introduces me as HER mentor, referencing what I have taught her about teaching and social media. Both of us feel as if we are both mentors and mentees to the other, and as a result we enjoy a wonderful, mutually beneficial relationship. Through our adventures we have also become close friends—an added bonus. Mentorship and friendship are ageless!

Another Story

We (Tori and I) have a traditional and reverse mentoring relationship as well. (Perhaps we should start calling this idea "mutual mentoring!") Tori was my student while she was at Fresno State, and I took her on as a mentee because I saw in her tremendous promise, drive, and professional passion. She held several leadership positions, including serving as the first executive director of our student-run public relations firm, and I mentored her in these roles. She also started her first PR business while in college, and I mentored her about client relations, fees, and more. After she graduated, we stayed in touch, and Tori worked as a subcontractor on a few of my professional projects. During all of this time, even though I held the title of "mentor" in our relationship, I learned just as much from Tori through her generosity as a reverse mentor. Through her encouragement and instruction I began actively engaging in social media (as a reasonably early adopter), and I continue to learn from her every week during our regular meetings about this-or-that technology trend or way of solving a challenge I have with the computer. I discovered online file sharing, online screen sharing, social media post scheduling, and many, many other fabulous tools and ideas via Tori's guidance. We continue to be each other's "soft place to fall" as it is so important for her (as a young entrepreneur) and me (as a forty-something who needs and wants to stay current) to have each other to ask questions of and to know that we'll get what we need in an atmosphere of support. We have also become close friends (which you'll notice is a common theme in strong mentor-mentee relationships!).

Traditional Mentoring

All relationships are different, and mentoring relationships are no exception. Most traditional mentoring falls into two categories—formal mentoring and informal mentoring. Formal mentoring is structured, with regular meetings and concrete agendas, feedback mechanisms, and more. An employer or club or association sometimes orchestrates formal mentoring, or it can be fostered by the individuals themselves (i.e., you reaching out to someone to be your mentor). Informal mentoring is less structured, but it could include some "regularity" depending on the individuals involved. Informal mentoring could be a supervisor counseling you before or after a presentation or meeting, or even a lunchroom conversation. Traveling with colleagues is a great opportunity for informal mentoring. I have had lovely visits with people in cars and planes and received quite a bit of counsel during these informal mentoring sessions.

How to Find a Mentor (or Another One)

Everyone wants a "made for TV movie" mentorship—the kind that is raw material for the Hallmark Channel or a heartfelt, iconic memoir like the amazing *Tuesdays with Morrie* by Mitch Albom. But how does that happen? And what can you do to increase your odds?

Let Your Need Be Known

I love the phrase, "Let your need be known." Coined by my friend and former colleague Bonni, it is something we all need to keep in mind for even more than just finding a mentor! If you don't let people know what you need, they can't help you find it. Tell everyone you know that you are looking for someone who can help you advance your career or passion. Ask people who they think you should reach out to and get their contact information. And then reach out! You can also pick peoples' brains to see what they think about some of your ideas regarding potential mentors. You can "prescreen" them to make sure that your thoughts about a person match what most others think about them as well.

Types of Mentors to Consider

Look around at those people who are respected in your industry and community. Look for those who are on the path to success and/or have enjoyed a successful and interesting career. Don't necessarily think that an older person is always the best mentor, but experience should definitely be part of the formula.

Start with Your Workplace

Sometimes the best mentors are right there in your office! Research opportunities for structured or unstructured mentoring where you work. Both your boss and your human resources people are good resources to explore these internal opportunities. Make sure you follow protocol. If one of the contacts you'd like to make is your boss's boss, make sure you keep your boss in the loop and explain why you want to pursue this meeting/relationship.

Get Back in Touch with Your Alma Mater

Reach out to your professors, advisers, and others at your college or university to see if they have any ideas about people you should connect with.

Often they will have many contacts that might be good matches for you. You might even want to ask if they have any projects you could help them on so you can build on your existing relationship. My favorite freelance subcontractors for my consulting projects are graduates of my program. I know the quality of their work, and working together more as colleagues provides the opportunity to create a whole new type of relationship.

A Story

David had a college professor who was well respected in the field of pavement engineering. He was a "pavement professor," and he taught at UC Davis and worked at a testing lab at UC Berkeley. Due to his connection at the testing lab, he worked with multiple contractors and firms, and he was held in high regard. He was more than happy to pass students' contact information along to contractors/firms whom he knew were looking for help. In that way, he was serving as a mentor for his students while also actively getting them in touch with other potential mentors and, in some cases, potential employers.

Be Visible

Just like many things in life, finding a mentor is a numbers game. The more people you meet, the better your odds of finding a mentor. Attend networking mixers. Visit with colleagues in the common areas at your workplace. Volunteer to help with community projects or events that you are passionate about. Get out there and meet some new people! Join professional associations (and smaller groups and/or committees within them). Being a part of small groups and working alongside others is the best way to get to know potential mentors (and give people a chance to get to know you and your fabulousness!).

Be Brave

Don't be afraid to reach out to your business idols. It may take a while, but it will surprise you who will actually say yes to a meeting or phone call. Do your research and be prepared, of course!

A Story

When Dawn moved to Los Angeles fifteen years ago she was encouraged to join the local chapter of the Public Relations Society of America. She was also told that she would receive the most benefit if she joined a committee and looked for more senior professionals that she could work alongside and learn from. About five years later, she decided to proactively ask three of the more senior members of the chapter if they'd be interested in being informal mentors to her. They were honored to be asked to support a junior public relations person, and over the years Dawn has continued to reach out occasionally to say hello, provide a referral, and ask for advice. One of her mentors has even supported the annual nonprofit event she does every year (Quality Time with PR Minds) through financial resources from his company. These three are the first people she would call if she were looking for her next job or if she reached a critical hurdle in her career and needed guidance. They've supported her in many ways, and she continues to be extremely glad she reached out to them and asked them to mentor her!

Research

Research your potential mentor(s). Find out about his or her background and what they may have to offer you. Doing this ahead of time will help avoid "bad matches" and steer you closer to people who can truly partner in your success.

Connect

Reach out and ask for an opportunity to buy your "prospect" a cup of coffee and spend a half hour with you to share some advice. If the meeting flops, you don't have to see this person again, and you can still call it a win by asking them for recommendations for others to talk to in order to build your network. If the meeting goes well, you could be on your way to having an amazing new mentor!

If You Get a "No"

If you reach out to someone and they either indirectly or directly let you know that they are not willing or unable to mentor you, ponder the possible reasons why before you take it personally. Perhaps it is as simple as not "clicking," or perhaps the person is truly too busy, or maybe even doesn't enjoy the role of mentoring. Find someone else who will encourage your growth.

A Story

A general manager of a local TV station passed up the chance to have a student as his intern/mentee because he thought she was too pushy and "in it for the glamour." She is now a correspondent for one of the major TV networks. Lessons: (1) Sometimes even seasoned pros misjudge folks. (2) If someone says "No," ask someone else—this woman obviously did!

Follow Up and Stay Connected

Establishing a mentoring relationship is very similar to good, basic networking. Make sure you send a thank-you note or email letting your new contact know how much you appreciated their time. Keep in touch with them via sending periodic news about you and also news or information they might enjoy or benefit from. Ask to schedule another meeting.

A Story

When Steve was the director of Corporate Communication for the San Francisco 49ers, many people (for obvious reasons) wanted to meet with him about possible jobs and/or mentoring. Steve has a very "pay it forward" approach to life, so he typically meets with anyone who reaches out to him. During a particularly busy period he met with seven young professionals. Steve didn't have any job openings at the time, and only two of the seven circled back and stayed in touch him. Several didn't even send a thank-you note for the meeting or followed up in any way. And only one worked at creating a relationship, sending articles that Steve might enjoy and requesting another meeting for a specific purpose. Steve went out of his way to help the latter young professional, and the others all missed out on applying for the opportunities that came up shortly after those meetings. In other meetings with potential mentees or interns or employees, Steve would be put off by the questions asked, like "How much interaction do you have with the players?" He wants to associate with (and eventually hire) professionals, not groupies. Lessons: (1) Do what you know you need to do. Write thank-you notes. Follow-up. Circle back. Stay in touch. It takes work, but the work is worth it! (2) Don't be a groupie.

Don't Be Shy

I tried to figure out a better way to subtitle this section, as we don't want anyone to interpret that we think there is anything wrong with shyness, because we don't. However, it is hard to meet people and develop relationships when you don't engage and talk to people. We know this is a very challenging thing for many, many people (ourselves included!). Sometimes it is hard to work up the courage. But you've got to do it. Put one foot in front of the other and walk across the room and introduce yourself.

One way to sort of "cheat" to overcome shyness is to ask others to introduce you to people. This takes some of the pressure and awkwardness out of the equation and can help you out. You can also "cheat" a little bit by having your first "conversation" with someone electronically—either via email or through a social network. This allows you to share information and get to know the person a little better, and they get to know you, as well, before you meet face to face. This increases everyone's comfort levels—always a good thing!

Don't Be a Stalker

My children joke a lot about "stalker status" regarding people they know on social media, and they also use the phrase *stalk much?* when referring to those that seem to "like" every post or update. And while they are using the term in a joking, nonthreatening way, it is important to note that social media and new technology has given us the opportunity to know way more about people than we used to. So be sure to create a healthy balance of reaching out and giving your would-be mentor space. You don't want to disturb them by liking every status they post or favoring every tweet. At first they might be flattered, but after a while they might worry why you don't have something else occupying your time.

Be Choosy

Your mentor should be someone that you are comfortable with, enjoy spending time with, and can help you with your career. Just like with dating, be selective and strategic regarding whom you approach and whom you spend your time with. Your time is valuable, and you want to make sure you are maximizing every bit of it!

Be Curious and Passionate

Mentors like to work with those who are passionate about their industry and excited about learning everything they can. Enthusiasm is contagious, and there is little that is more fun than feeding the passion and enthusiasm of someone who wants to excel at their craft, especially if it's a craft that you are just as passionate about. This is the formula for a winning mentoring relationship!

Most People Are Honored to Be Mentors

While yes, being a mentor takes time and energy that some people truly just don't have, most people are honored to be asked to be a mentor, and most will say yes if at all possible with respect to their busy schedules. It's an honor to coach and help shape someone's career, and it's a gift for you to give someone that honor. This is important to remember!

You Can Have More Than One Mentor

There is no rule that you can only have one mentor, or even that you can only have one mentor at a time. Different people approach things differently, so use this fact to your advantage. You might want to consider reaching out to more than one person to mentor you.

How to Be an Amazing Mentee

Random note: the word *mentee* is so goofy to me. It reminds me of the word *manatee*, which, probably not so ironically, happens to be one of my favorite animals (which is goofy to you, I'm sure). Regardless, it's the word we've chosen to use for this chapter. Some people use the term *protégé*, but our interpretation of that word is that it represents a much stronger relationship than most people have with their mentors, and it also includes a very clearly defined subordinate relationship, something we do not advocate. Also, *protégé* implies that the person on the receiving end of the information/being mentored is receiving it only so that they may one day take their mentor's place. However, as stated prior, the mentor/mentee relationship is not limited to just you and your supervisor! So *mentee* it is . . . (if you think of a better term, please let us know!)

First of all—be excited! Having a mentor is a tremendous gift. Don't forget to enjoy it!

Set Expectations

Be up front with the type of guidance and help you need and want. Clear goals lead to goal accomplishment! Share your goals (in writing), and create a plan to make sure both of you have a shared vision and you both stay on track. Be sure to include some notes regarding things you want to learn more about and your longer-term visions for your professional life (i.e., where do you see yourself in three years? Five years? Ten years?).

Some things you might want to include in your "mentoring wish list":

- Resources—what books, blogs, workshops, conferences, and other resources does your mentor recommend?

- Skills—what should you learn and/or improve? And how can you do so?

- Networking—who else should you be connecting with?

- Attendance—are there any opportunities for you to go to things with your mentor to learn or observe?

- Feedback—as you share your successes and challenges, what can you do differently and better?

- Stories—what experiences has your mentor had in the areas that you are struggling with?

Take and Maintain Initiative

Since your mentoring relationship is primarily for your benefit, know that the burden is on you to maintain the relationship. This means that you need to take the lead on scheduling and other items. Be sure you make it easy and convenient for your mentor to meet with you and connect with you. Ask for "homework" or things to work on in between your get-togethers. Be constantly thinking of new ways to help each other grow.

A Story

I have a student who is very bright and ambitious. When she found out I was going to be on sabbatical the semester she was scheduled to take her senior "capstone" class from me (therefore not having me as an instructor for the course), she immediately asked to work on another project with me. Anything, she said; she just wanted to have the opportunity to learn more. While I didn't have anything specific in mind at that moment, I told her yes anyway, and I figured out a way for she and I to work together the semester before my sabbatical. Her confidence and dedication encouraged me to figure out a way.

Be Flexible

Try not to get upset or offended if your mentor needs to cut short or reschedule a meeting. Things happen, and it is a good relationship builder to be "cool" with changes in plans. However, if it happens frequently, it might be a sign that your relationship might not be a priority for your mentor, and you might want to look elsewhere for more frequent guidance. After all, you can still keep in loose touch with the person with "scheduling issues."

Also, regarding your goals and objectives for your mentoring experience, don't be so rigid that you prevent yourself from experiencing and benefiting from your mentoring relationship in ways that aren't in your plan. Be open to getting involved in things your mentor is working on—offer to help!

Discuss How to Communicate

Use the method of communication preferred by your mentor, not you. Your mentor may love or hate phones, emails, texts, or instant messages. Ask them how they want you to communicate with them and also what boundaries they want you to have (e.g., is it OK to communicate in the evenings or on weekends? What about early mornings?)

While getting together in person is typically the best way to create, maintain, and grow a relationship, don't discount the use of technology. Skyping or FaceTime might be great ways to "see" your mentor when you can't physically be in the same room. We recommend these technologies over the phone as there is so much added value when you can talk "face to face."

Note: Tori and I use Skype for all of our meetings as we live in different parts of the state and only see each other a few times per year "in person." However, we truly feel as if we always see each other because of this technology. Never underestimate the power of a virtual "high-five" or even a virtual champagne toast!

Be Yourself

Being authentic is critical to a healthy relationship, and frankly it makes your life easier as well. Be the best version of yourself, of course, as that's what you want to bring to all areas of your life, but please be who you are. Sharing the "real you" allows your mentor to help you in the fullest way possible.

Take It Seriously

If you are not "all in" your mentoring relationship, don't be in it. It's not fair to your mentor (or to you) if you are not completely invested. Here are ways to prove to your mentor that you are committed.

- Be on time! Or, better yet, be a few minutes early. You want your mentor to know that you will always be there when you are supposed to be. (This will help them be more prompt as they have the pressure of knowing you will always be there on time!)

- Have something to take notes on. It is annoying to have to give your mentee a pad of paper or pen. Have those things with you at all times, even if you typically take notes on an electronic device; you never know when the battery might die or wireless Internet might not be available or working.

- Practice active listening (lean in, nod occasionally, make good eye contact).

Tip: If eye contact freaks you out, or is difficult for you, practice nose contact. People cannot tell if you are looking at their nose or their eyes. Try it today—it's a masterful trick!

- Have your "homework" (whatever that may be) completed in a thorough manner. Don't bring excuses to your meetings with your mentor. Get it done. Show that this relationship is important to you. Follow through. Flakiness is a relationship (and brand) killer.

- Put away your phone! While your friends and colleagues your age are used to and/or OK with your interactions on your phone being a part of spending time with you, your mentor will most likely find it rude and incredibly annoying. Even if your mentor is addicted to his/her phone, put yours away.

- Consider always dressing professionally when you are meeting with your mentor. Even if it's casual Friday or an occasion that you wouldn't typically dress up, do it anyway. There is a psychological boost to "looking the part." (I believe this so much that I tell everyone who is going to do a phone interview to dress up anyway, as it helps you be in the right frame of mind. Dressing the part does the same thing.)

- Watch your language. Even if you are comfortable with your mentor, don't swear or use slang during your conversations. Slang and profanity harms your brand, and it makes you appear less intelligent than you are.

- Use good manners. Don't interrupt. Hold doors open for people. Stand and greet people when they enter the room.

Be Prepared

Make sure you research and come prepared for each meeting with your mentor. Have specific questions and things you want to discuss so you both maximize your time together. Don't EVER "wing it" with your mentor. The more you respect someone's time, the more they will respect you. Most likely, you'll be responsible for leading the sessions with your mentor. If your mentor wants to lead, hopefully he or she will let you know. Better yet—ask if he/she would like to lead your meetings.

Tip: Kristie, a wonderful media professional I know, had the opportunity to be mentored by a high-ranking executive in her organization. To be prepared, she set up a Google Alert for her mentor (www.Google.com/alerts) so that she was always in the loop regarding her activities and achievements. This enabled her to have more meaningful conversations with her mentor and helped her be as current as possible in her mentor's world.

Give Feedback and Share Success

Be sure to circle back and let your mentor know what happened when you took his/her advice. Also be sure to keep your mentor(s) in the loop regarding your career successes. They want to know, of course, and these bits of news also let them know that you are growing based on your relationship, something that is gratifying to both of you. Especially as the years go by, and you perhaps aren't in as close touch with your mentor, send them messages and notes that keep them apprised of your "wins."

Show Appreciation

Don't forget to let your mentor know you are grateful. Thank them for their time at the end of your meetings, and also periodically send handwritten notes of appreciation. In this era of electronic communication, a handwritten note stands out and really makes an impact. An occasional gift card (for coffee or Amazon or something, not a high dollar amount) is also a wonderful token of thanks. Buy your mentor coffee or lunch on occasion (he or she will fuss, but they will also be touched and appreciate it!). One of my students made me cookies as a thank you, and another made me cupcakes; both gifts were so appreciated because of the thought and kindness behind them. Another student, knowing that I love Diet Pepsi, brought me several bottles as a thank you for helping her with a significant professional challenge. It is not the cost of the mark of appreciation, it truly is the thought behind it that counts. And it counts BIG! Think of what your mentor would truly value based on his/her likes and preferences. Listen to what they talk about enjoying. Look around their office for clues. Observe what they eat and drink. It makes people feel special when you customize!

In addition, shout-outs on social media are incredibly welcome. Everyone likes to be thanked publically, and social media is this century's best way to do that.

Weigh All Advice Carefully

Your mentor(s) will probably be amazing, and most of the time will give you perfect advice. But sometimes, something they advise you to do might not "feel" right. Trust your gut, always!

Ask for Honest Feedback and Learn

I tell my students, especially those who want to be better public speakers, to video themselves and then watch the video with someone who provides honest feedback. This person is typically not their mother, as moms will usually tell their children how wonderful they are and not perhaps point out some "areas of opportunity." I encourage my students to find someone who is able to help them identify those areas of opportunity.

This is what your mentor needs to be for you—a contributor of honest, constructive feedback. You might not want to hear some of the feedback, but try to take everything your mentor shares with you and process it, weighing its importance as well as your perception of its "fairness," and use it to make you better. We are all imperfect, and we can all improve, if we choose to take feedback and use it in the way it was intended.

Observe

You can learn just as much (if not more) from your mentors by observing their actions. Watch how they interact with others, how they handle stressful situations, and try to model the behaviors you observe as being successful.

A Story

I was VERY young (in both age and maturity) when I started my first "real" job in a public relations firm. I tended to talk too quickly on the phone, and I was also a bit awkward during staff meetings. My supervisor took me aside and encouraged me to watch the firm's female partner and try to model her behavior. "Watch Christi," she said. "Do what she does." Up to that point I had never really thought about learning from people through observation. But I took her advice and watched how Christi spoke, presented herself, and interacted with both colleagues and clients. I knew I didn't want to (nor could I) become her "clone," but I did want to fold her wonderful example into my professional life. To this day, I still consider her when I'm not sure how to approach something. A solid role model is a powerful ally!

Another Story

One of Chris's first bosses was a wonderful mentor, and he learned much from her through their formal and informal conversations. However, he believes that he learned the most through watching her. No matter what was going on, she was calm. She always had a smile on her face and was always moving the organization forward. Another of Chris's mentors taught him (through his actions) to be thoughtful and strategic about everything that he does. This mentor modeled how to be ethical about decision making without being "in your face" about it.

Say Yes!

Try to take advantage of all the opportunities your mentor gives to you. When you are asked to attend events or work on projects or meet people—try to say yes as much as possible! And be willing to step out of your comfort zone. This is often when we learn the most!

Invite Yourself

Offer to attend meetings or events with your mentor. I always tell my students you can learn a lot "through osmosis."

A Story

David's boss offhandedly mentioned a meeting he had with a contractor David might be working with in the future. David had not met the contractor before, so he asked, "Would it be good for me to go as well?" His boss said, "I think so. Have you met (name of contractor)? If nothing else, it would be good for you to meet (name of another person at the meeting)." Even if David didn't end up working on the project, he got to expand his network, and by taking initiative and attending, he probably increased the odds of being given the project. Win!

Help Your Mentor

Even though you are the mentee, you still have a lot to offer your mentor. Are there people you know that they could benefit from knowing as well? Is there information you have access to that could help them move their projects and career forward? (Be sure to respect all ethical and confidentiality considerations, of course!) Read on for more about this idea in the section about reverse mentoring later in this chapter.

Use Your Mentor Appropriately

Your mentor can help you brainstorm, provide contacts and advice, and perhaps even help you with skill building. However, it is best to remember that your mentor is not your parent or counselor, and usually noncareer-related problems are best not included. If you and your mentor develop the kind of relationship in which discussing those things is appropriate, then by all means go ahead and do so, but most people are best served by treating mentors as great opportunities to form solid PROFESSIONAL relationships. Be judicious with your favors and requests. Make them count.

Remember That You "Represent" Your Mentor (and Vice Versa)

Especially if you are in a situation in which many people are aware of your mentoring relationship, remember that your behaviors will then reflect on your mentor. Work hard to honor that reality and make your mentor proud, not embarrassed.

But remember that your mentor also represents you, and if, as your relationship progresses, you are not comfortable with being associated with your mentor, don't be afraid to sever the relationship. You can formally do this, or informally let the relationship fade. If you chose the informal route and you are confronted, it will be important to honestly yet kindly let your mentor know that you have decided to go in a different direction. You can say (or write) something like, "While I appreciate you reaching out, I'm actually working closely with another mentor now. I wish you the best."

Ask WHY

The "what" and "how" are, of course, so important to being a successful professional, but the "WHY" is often the most critical piece. Be sure to ask your mentor WHY all the time, as that is where your deep learning and understanding will take place.

Be Honest

Tell your mentor what you are struggling with, the mistakes you make, and other important issues. Your mentor can't help you if you don't share. Saying everything is "fine" won't build your relationship. Your mentor expects you to have advice that you need and situations for them to help you with. That's why they are there!

Respect Confidences

A great mentor will share all kinds of stories, many of which are meant "for your ears only." Be sure not to violate the wonderful trust your mentor has shown by sharing those types of stories.

A Story

Not too long ago, David's mentor shared with him an amazing, shocking, hilarious story. It was by far one of the best stories he had ever heard in his life. And he didn't share it with us, because it was told to him in confidence. (And yes, we were bummed.) The moral of the story: Not all stories are for sharing—the more your mentor opens up to you, the more it means he/she trusts you. Don't ruin that trust by sharing some of their confidential tips, tricks, and stories with the world!

Ask the Dumb Question (the Smart Way)

When you were little, and perhaps even as recently as during college, you may have heard that there are no dumb questions. Well, we are sorry to share with you that this is not true. Especially in the professional world, asking a dumb question can really harm your credibility.

I never tell my students that there are no dumb questions. And even though I don't chastise them when they ask one, I may remember what they asked, and that information goes into my "file" of information about how I perceive that person.

Yes, your mentor should be your "soft place to fall," as referenced above, but you also want them to remain your champion. Ask questions, lots of them, but if you have a question that you think might be "dumb" (i.e., perhaps you should know the answer already), think about how you ask it, and consider doing some prep ahead of time. Do some research, and if you still need some help or clarification, ask! Here are some ways to couch your "dumb" questions:

- I am sure that I knew this at one point, but I can't remember how to . . . do you know?
- I've read that . . . but I'm still a little fuzzy on this idea. What are your thoughts?

You can also call yourself out by saying something like, "I'm certain that I should know this already, but . . ." or "I know that folks say there are no dumb questions, but I'm sure this is one, but I feel comfortable enough with you to ask it anyway . . ."

The bottom line here is to use your mentor as a resource, but don't get lazy about it.

Share Your Thoughts and Ideas

If you have a great idea for your mentor—share it! As you read above, the best mentoring relationships are "two-way streets" in which both people learn and grow from each other.

Assess

Periodically, have an assessment conversation with your mentor. Ask him/her if they are satisfied with how things are going and ask for suggestions for improvement. And share the same information with them.

Take It to the Next Level

One of my favorite ideas in this area comes from my friend Jill, who shared with me that she has a personal "Board of Directors," a group of people who are diverse in many ways—expertise, industries, ages, and more. These are people she relies on for guidance and advice. As you grow in your career, we highly encourage you to consider this idea. People will move in and out of your life, including mentors, but there are some folks who you will really want to keep. You may choose to tell them that you have "appointed" them to your personal Board, or you may keep their "membership" to yourself.

How to Be a Great Traditional Mentor

Because we know that in addition to practicing reverse mentoring (more about this later) you will more than likely also become a traditional mentor as you move throughout your career, here are some ideas for being an amazing mentor. These tips can also remind you to appreciate and value your own mentor(s)!

Note from Tori: You might be surprised how quickly you turn around and become a mentor! It happened for me when I was still in college and was able to figure out social media, blogging, and personal websites before they were widespread. These topics weren't part of our curriculum at the time (it was all very new), and so I became a mentor to others around me who wanted to learn how to use the sites and showcase their brand and accomplishments online. As soon as I graduated, I also mentored my sister through her college career. I'm young, but I've been through more than many others my age, and so I am able to have mentoring relationships with others who are close to my age.

Assess Yourself

Think about why you are considering being a mentor. Make sure that mentoring fits with your strategic plan for your life and career. While traditional mentoring is primarily designed to serve the mentee, the relationship should serve you as well. For example, being a mentor is a fabulous way to improve your leadership skills and help your professional growth. Mentors often report that they believe they get just as much—if not more—from their mentees than their mentees gain from them!

Be Committed

Being a mentor takes time and energy (and some patience!), and if you don't have these things right now, don't commit. A half-hearted effort, while still perhaps slightly noble, doesn't serve either of you very well. Consider whether you are committing to the short term or long term. Both types of mentoring work well, but be honest with yourself and your mentee about what you are envisioning for this relationship. Honesty is the foundation for all solid partnerships!

Set Expectations

Let your mentee know what you are able/willing to do for them. Share your preferred method of communication, and also how much time you are able to give her/him. If there is something that you feel you can learn from your mentee, be open about it and put that item on your "agenda" (whether you have a formal one or not). Joint projects are often great ways for mentees and mentors to work together and learn from each other. Think about whether you have a project that would stretch your mentee and allow them to grow and/or would enable you to learn from your mentee as well.

Model Your Expectations

Whatever you want in your mentee, be that yourself (i.e., prompt, attentive, prepared, not glued to your phone, etc.). As we have discussed, people learn a lot from us through observation (and we can learn a lot from them!). In fact, we believe it is one of the best teachers.

Be Accessible

It shouldn't be difficult for your mentee to get a hold of you. Your mentee should, of course, respect the boundaries you have set, but they should be on the list of people you are most responsive to, even if you are busy.

Discuss the "Intangibles"

In addition to support and guidance of industry issues and specific work projects, make sure your discussions and instruction also include what sports commentators call the "intangibles"—work ethic, initiative, attitude, the importance of relationships, and more.

Help Mistakes Turn into Lessons

We have all probably learned more from our mistakes than our successes, and this is something to remember as we are counseling our mentees. When things go wrong, which they most certainly will, it is a gift to help someone work through the evaluation process so learning can happen based on the mistake(s). If you can do this for your mentee, you will be of tremendous value to him/her.

Listen

Yes, you are the "sage" in the relationship, and it will be important for you to share your wisdom and advice. But be sure to also spend time listening to your mentee. This will help you learn what they need and also might help you grow and learn as well.

Be Willing to Learn from Your Mentee

Acting like you "know it all" won't help either of you. Your mentee will enjoy teaching you things, so let him/her! You will learn, and they will gain confidence and feel proud. It's a win-win!

Know What They Need from You

Mentees need perspective from you, as well as objectivity. You can help them by being a resource. Your mentee also needs you to be authentic. Show them the real you. As we discussed above, authenticity is key to all successful relationships. Just because you think you "should" do something with your mentee, don't do it if you don't want to or if you don't think it would be of benefit. This is your unique relationship with your mentee, and you both get to write the rules!

Don't forget about patience. Your mentee will certainly do things that cause you to shake your head (literally or figuratively), but take a deep breath and remember that if they did everything perfectly—they wouldn't need you!

Consider Your Mentee Your Peer, Not Your Subordinate

Introduce them to everyone. Walk beside them. When a relationship is crafted more as peers, people behave differently, and we believe that difference is of benefit to all involved.

Be a Connector

Help your mentee network. Introduce him/her to people you know that they might enjoy meeting and/or could help them move forward. Advancement is dependent on relationships, so help your mentee establish the relationships they need.

Be a Guide, Not a Dictator

Help your mentee "get there" instead of telling them what to do and where to go. The best mentors help their mentees develop and fine-tune their own critical-thinking skills and decision-making processes. Ask probing questions like:

- What do you think your options are in this situation?

- What decision are you leaning toward?

- How do you think you'd handle this situation five years from now?

And when offering advice, instead of taking a "this is what you should do" approach, consider phrases like:

- Have you thought about doing this?

- This might be a good option for you . . .

- I have had experience with doing it this way . . . that might work for you as well . . .

Instead of "I Told You So . . ."

If your mentee doesn't take your advice, or takes only part of your advice and then has some negative consequences, please resist the urge to say, "I told you so." Be honored that your mentee had the courage to come to you and share that they suffered from not taking your advice. Instead, try to teach them the process of evaluation and making sure the same mistake doesn't happen again. Also, encourage them to move on. As my colleague Peter likes to say, "Just draw the line in the sand and say 'that was then, this is now.' And then move on."

A Story

When David graduated from college and got a job, a year or so later a temporary opening popped up in his company. He had a chance to go work it and gain some additional experience, and he was thrilled at the opportunity, but first he had to find a temporary replacement to fill in for him. As it turned out, a college friend of his who had just graduated (about a year behind him) was looking for work. It was temporary, but it was better than nothing, so he took it. Before David left for the temporary assignment, he walked him through everything and "showed him the ropes." He was energetic and ready to work, but David advised him that in a few distinct areas, areas that were nonpriorities, his overeagerness would in fact end up overtaking him.

David told him that an hour spent working today in this area would translate to three to four times the amount of time in the future, so while it may start off slow (and he may have a lot of free time to begin with), to take on too much at once would result in being significantly overburdened later (and would leave less free time to work on the real priorities).

Well, he didn't listen to David. He took on everything he could to fill his time RIGHT NOW, and, sure enough, a week or so later he was swamped. The work he had started had snowballed, as David had warned. When David caught up with him, he could see in his eyes the "I know you were right" look; David didn't have to say anything. Moral of the story: you don't have to kick someone when he's down. Often, when your mentee doesn't take your advice and ends up in over his or her head, they already know it.

Pass Along Compliments

As others recognize the awesomeness of your mentee, be sure to share those compliments with them. My favorite thing is to tell one of my mentees, colleagues, or students that someone was talking nicely behind their back. In fact, I have a policy that I always share compliments that are given to others when they are not in the room.

Be Present

Give your mentee your full attention when you are with him/her. Put away your phone, stop checking messages, and focus on your conversation. Given how most people behave these days, just this small habit will do wonders for the quality of your relationships and also encourage others to want to be involved with you.

Be Open

Whether this means to literally have your door open and welcome others into your office space or just having the "aura" of being open and willing to help others, being "open" will attract others to you.

Note: You may have overexperienced this, so be judicious with your openness so you are not overwhelmed. Boundaries—the most important component of twenty-first-century success!

You Don't Have to Know it All

Don't be nervous that your mentee will expect you to know everything. He or she doesn't. In fact, you will be more endearing to them if you don't! And you don't have to know exactly how to solve all of your mentee's problems. Listen, care, encourage reflection and critical thought, and help them find the answers they need.

In class, I actually enjoy it when I don't know the answer to a student's question, as this gives me a chance to learn as well. I make a note, and ask them to do the same, and we circle back next time. Or, I have someone look up the answer right then and there, and we all learn in "real time."

Share About When You Goofed

Don't be shy about sharing your big and little blunders. It helps "humanize" you to your mentee, and it also helps them also learn from your (painful) lessons. Please, tell it like it is. One of the things I promise my students on the first day of class each semester is that I'll be honest with them. I teach in the context of the real world, not a fantasyland perfect world that they will never see. Your mentees deserve that level of honesty as well.

Champion Your Mentee

Be free and generous with your public praise and encouragement of your mentee. (And they will do the same for you!)

Stretch Your Mentee

Especially if you are in a supervisor/subordinate relationship with your mentee, don't be afraid to give them tasks that will stretch them. Often by giving someone a little "more than they can chew," we give them an opportunity to grow and shine!

A Story

When Steve was a junior in college working for the University of Wyoming's sports information office, his mentor gave him the gargantuan task of organizing the NCAA skiing championships, an unheard-of responsibility for someone who was still a student. Steve and his mentor held regular progress meetings, and the mentor was always responsive and helpful, but the task fell squarely on Steve's shoulders. The event was a tremendous success, and one of the competing school's public information officers complimented Steve and started asking questions about his background. "Where were you before Wyoming?" he asked. "High school," Steve replied. The PIO couldn't believe that a college student—an intern—had pulled off this huge event. He was so impressed that he wrote to Steve's mentor (boss) about his approval of how things were handled at the championship. Steve's mentor believe in him and gave him a task that he knew would stretch Steve—and Steve responded.

Check In Regularly

Don't let your mentee be the one who always reaches out. Make sure you are also taking the time and effort to connect, especially in between "meetings."

Be Honest (with Kindness)

Provide both positive and negative feedback to your mentee. If you think they could have done something better or need to improve, share your honest feelings in a kind and supportive way. Being told you are great all the time isn't always the most helpful sort of feedback.

It Is OK to Walk Away

If your mentee violates your trust or behaves unprofessionally to the point at which you don't want to be associated with them, know that it is OK to sever the relationship. It would be best for your mentee if you do this formally so they can use it as a learning experience.

Reverse Mentoring

Reverse mentoring is a fascinating concept that is really gaining popularity in this age of dynamic technology and expanding social media networks. You have probably already recognized that you might know a lot more about computers or the Internet or smartphones or social media than many people who are more seasoned and experienced than you are. And you might have also noticed that the more seasoned and experienced professionals are in need of this knowledge. This phenomenon has set the stage for an unprecedented and growing amount of reverse mentoring, where the younger, less experienced professional mentors the older, more experienced one.

Just as with traditional mentoring, reverse mentoring can be both formal and informal, and it can be facilitated by an employer or happen organically. These relationships can be ongoing, intermittent, or one-time experiences.

What is VERY different, however, is the dynamics of the relationship. Because reverse mentoring is, by definition, nontraditional, there are some "issues" that many people need to work through in order for it to be successful. First of all, it is important for you, the reverse mentor, to know that sometimes the person you are mentoring will be reluctant to admit that he/she doesn't know it all. It is often awkward for the veteran to recognize that he/she doesn't have all of the answers. Also, sometimes the person you are mentoring will have anxiety about the "subject" of your mentoring (social media, technology, etc.), so that needs to be taken into consideration as well. On the flip side, you might not have a handle on the strategy or context for the "subject" that you are mentoring about, and so this makes things tricky as well.

A Story

When David's dad first started his job some thirty years ago (or whatever it was), he recalls being in the lunchroom his first week. There, a bunch of old-timers were complaining about the same thing: "I just don't know. It's changing the industry!" "I can't figure it out. It's too complicated and I'm too old for this [stuff], I might as well just retire." "If this is the way things are going with this company and this industry, I might as well roll over dead now!" The funny part of this story: they were talking about voicemail. The lesson: there will always be some newer, more advanced technology or strategy, or something that some youngster is going to know more about than you.

The keys to reverse mentoring include commitment and sensitivity. There needs to be a commitment by both parties to work together and sensitivity on both sides of the equation—yours to recognize that learning from you might be new or uncomfortable for an industry veteran, and theirs to be able to recognize that you are offering something of significant value.

You, your mentee, and your organization can set the stage for success by setting up and encouraging a culture of learning in all directions: top-down, bottom-up, and side-to-side. When people are used to learning and teaching in a myriad of models, awkwardness and defensiveness diminishes significantly!

Just as with other forms of mentoring, the articulation of specific goals and expectations leads to success. A genuine desire to learn must be present in your mentee. Just going through the motions and/or closed-mindedness doesn't help anyone.

Location is a little more important with reverse mentoring, as sometimes your mentee might be more comfortable in his/her office so they can have both privacy and still maintain the "authority" or "senior" role. Patience is also important, as you will probably need to share some lessons more than once in order for them to "stick." While you, as a "digital native," will pick things up in the technology space quickly, your mentee, who grew up in a different time with different tools, might take more time. Share, check for understanding, and be ready to repeat. Slow the pace significantly; this experience will be different than sharing something about technology with someone your own age. Be sensitive to vocabulary as well. Words that you use all the time might not be as familiar to your mentee. Ask if definitions are needed, and try to have your definitions be as jargon-free as possible (or you might have to define your definition!). And, while, yes, you are the "mentor" in a reverse mentoring scenario, being humble will go a long way. Acting as if you know it all and/or your mentee is slow or stupid will lead you nowhere. Be overly respectful.

Note: Many of the successful reverse mentors we have interviewed report that often their mentees enjoy reminiscing as part of the experience. You might expect to hear about "the good old days" before current technology. If you expect these stories and just go with it and listen, you might even enjoy them!

In all of this, be proud that you are able to share with a seasoned professional and help them learn and grow. This is a wonderful gift that you are able to share, and you should most certainly feel good about it!

Colleague Mentoring

You can use many of the tips and advice above for peer or colleague mentoring, and we mention it here so you will remember to think of mentoring in a myriad of ways and directions. As you grow in your career it is our hope that you will experience all kinds of mentoring, and also offer to be a mentor, as you have much to give!

CHEAT SHEET

- Why you need a mentor

- Traditional mentoring

- How to find a mentor (or another one)
  - Let your need be known
  - Types of mentors to consider
  - Start with your workplace
  - Get back in touch with your alma mater
  - Be visible
  - Be brave
  - Research
  - Connect
  - If you get a "no"
  - Follow up and stay connected
  - Don't be shy
  - Don't be a stalker
  - Be choosy
  - Be curious and passionate
  - Most people are honored to be mentors
  - You can have more than one mentor

- How to be an amazing mentee
  - Set expectations
  - Take and maintain initiative
  - Be flexible
  - Discuss how to communicate
  - Be yourself
  - Take it seriously
  - Be prepared
  - Give feedback and share success
  - Show appreciation
  - Weigh all advice carefully

- Ask for honest feedback and learn
- Observe
- Say yes!
- Invite yourself
- Help your mentor
- Use your mentor appropriately
- Remember that you "represent" your mentor (and vice versa)
- Ask WHY
- Be honest
- Respect confidences
- Ask the dumb question (the smart way)
- Share your thoughts and ideas
- Assess
- Take it to the next level

- How to be a great traditional mentor
  - Assess yourself
  - Be committed
  - Set expectations
  - Model your expectations
  - Be accessible
  - Discuss the "intangibles"
  - Help mistakes turn into lessons
  - Listen
  - Be willing to learn from your mentee
  - Know what they need from you
  - Consider your mentee your peer, not your subordinate
  - Be a connector
  - Be a guide, not a dictator
  - Instead of "I told you so . . ."
  - Pass along compliments
  - Be present
  - Be open
  - You don't have to know it all
  - Share about when you goofed
  - Champion your mentee
  - Stretch your mentee

- ○ Check in regularly
- ○ Be honest (with kindness)
- ○ It is OK to walk away

- Reverse Mentoring

- Colleague Mentoring

Resources and References

Many thanks to my research colleague, Dr. Doug Swanson (California State University, Fullerton), for his tireless contributions and leadership in our work regarding reverse mentoring in public relations. Much of what we have read and discovered is relevant to this chapter.

Sources and Further Reading Regarding Reverse Mentoring

Calvelli, D. "The ROI of Reverse Mentoring." *Philadelphia Business Journal*, January 18, 2013. Retrieved from http://www.bizjournals.com/philadelphia/print-edition/2013/01/18/the-roi-of-reverse-mentoring.html?page=all.

Crisp, G., and I. Cruz. "Mentoring College Students: A Critical Review of the Literature between 1990 and 2007." *Research in Higher Education* 50 (2009): 525–45.

Hays, B. A., and D. J. Swanson. "Prevalence and Success of Reverse Mentoring in Public Relations." *Public Relations Journal* 5 (2011), 4. Retrieved from http://www.prsa.org/Intelligence/PRJournal/Documents/2011HaysSwanson.pdf.

———. "Using Reverse and Traditional Mentoring to Develop New Media Skills and Maintain Social Order in the Public Relations Workplace." In *New Media and Public Relations*, 2nd ed. Edited by S. C. Duhe. New York: Peter Lang, 2012.

Management Mentors. "The 411 on All Things Mentoring Related." Retrieved from http://www.management-mentors.com/resources/corporate-mentoring-programs-faqs/.

Peroune, D. "Tacit Knowledge in the Workplace: The Facilitating Role of Peer Relationships." *Journal of European Industrial Training* 31, no. 1 (2007): 244.

Pyle, K. "Youth Are the Present." *Telephony* 246 (2005): 40.

White, C., A. Vane, and G. Stafford. "Internal Communication, Information Satisfaction, and Sense of Community: The Effect of Personal Influence." *Journal of Public Relations Research* 22, no. 1 (2010): 65–84.

Ideas for Further Reading (Thank you, Dr. Swanson!)

Carroll, M. *Awake at Work: 35 Practical Buddhist Principles for Discovering Clarity and Balance in the Midst of Work's Chaos*. Boston: Shambhala Publications, 2006.

McRaney, D. *You Are Not So Smart*. New York: Gotham Books, 2011.

Tan, C. M. *Search Inside Yourself: The Unexpected Path to Achieving Success, Happiness (and World Peace)*. New York: HarperCollins, 2012.

LIFELONG LEARNING
Betsy

Thankfully this is not as common as it used to be, but people used to celebrate the end of their college (or even high school) years by saying they were "done" with learning—the old "no more teachers, no more books" approach. Well, we are sure that you have figured out that this is no longer the case—especially if you would like to advance past entry-level anything.

That said, the opportunities for lifelong learning are essentially limitless, and, as such, they can sometimes be extremely overwhelming.

This chapter is all about ways you can feasibly continue your lifelong learning while maintaining the balance that we've tried so hard to help you achieve via this book!

While you can learn in probably a million different ways, for "ease of use" we will divide your lifelong learning opportunities into two categories—informal and formal. We will define formal learning as opportunities to learn in traditional ways, such as taking a class or attending a conference or working toward an advanced degree. Formal learning includes some sort of "instructor"—either in person or virtually—that leads or at least points to the knowledge that will be obtained. Informal learning is everything else—all that is not structured or clearly labeled.

Hopefully it is obvious that both types of lifelong learning are important to your success. The more you learn, typically, the more successful you will become!

Informal Learning

Be Open

You may have heard the term *know-it-all*, or at the very least be repulsed by the sound of this phrase. Those of us who think that we have nothing left to learn are typically the ones who need to learn the most (yet another manifestation of karma or Murphy's Law or however you would like to phrase it!). Trust us. It won't be long before you find yourself in a reverse mentorship, with some young person you just hired teaching YOU how to work the latest technological do-hickey (as talked about in the previous chapter).

It's best to be OPEN—open to the idea of always being able to learn something new. This doesn't mean that we want you to act as if you are clueless, but it does mean that you may want to adopt an attitude of willingness to add knowledge to your brain at any time. In fact, becoming a "knowledge junkie"—someone who gets excited about and "feeds" on new learning—will serve you well.

You might be wondering what "being open" looks like. If you are open to learning, you:

- listen to others when they talk

- conduct research (at least for a few minutes) before doing anything new, or doing anything you haven't done in a while

- ask for thoughts and input from others

- read—a lot, both in quantity and in diversity of topics

- ask questions

Observe

Observation is one of our greatest informal learning tools. You can learn a lot from watching others. You might find things you want to emulate, and/or you will see things you want to never, ever, ever do.

This is especially important if you are one who is typically the center of attention. Take a step back every once it a while and just watch. And listen. And observe how others respond to the words and actions of those around them. This is POWERFUL learning—and it's free!

Collect Smart People

Obviously I don't mean this literally, but I like the collection metaphor here because I like to think of the smart people in my life as "mine"—as in their brains are available to me when I need them (and mine is available to them, too, of course, as helpful or unhelpful as that is!).

I am sure there is evidence that proves this, but logic and intuition (two of my favorite things) should tell you that being with smart people makes you smarter!

Some people are reluctant to hang out with smart people for fear of appearing not as smart, or even dumb. And while occasionally one of your "smart friends" may outshine you in one area or another, no one is an expert at everything, and you will always benefit from being with smart people in a minimum of two ways. First, there is "guilt by association." If you are known to be with smart people, people will assume that you are smart as well. And perception is reality, right? Also, there is the adage that is something like "A rising tide raises all ships." What we interpret this to mean is that you are going to bring your "A" game to a conversation with smart folks, and this helps us not become intellectually lazy.

Surf the Web

While we feel a little silly even including this section in this book, as you, a digital native, are probably thinking "duh!"—it is important to talk about and remember the amazing and overwhelming information source we have at our fingertips (or thumbs!) essentially all the time.

Associations, forums, and groups can be wonderful resources for you online about just about any topic. These communities tend to be more self-policing than other places on the Web, therefore providing more credible and accurate information. You can also subscribe to blogs and newsletters so information comes straight to you!

A word of caution is warranted here, however. As you know, just because it is online doesn't make it true. Make sure you are both critical and cautious about trusting information you find online. We advocate using the "5 W's" approach:

- WHO: Who is providing the information? Why should you believe that they are credible?

- WHAT: What type of information are they providing, and does it make sense for them to provide this type of information?

- WHEN: How recent is the information? Is the "when" important?

- WHERE: Where are they located? This may be important, or it may be completely unimportant, depending on the type of information. For example, if you are researching local laws on a specific topic, someone from out of state or out of the country might not be the most credible source of information.

- WHY: Why are they providing this information?

Evaluating information this way will help you make better decisions regarding what you find online.

Read and Examine Offline

Books, magazines, and other types of non-website-or-social-media reading are also important to informal learning. Whether you are a paper person or a pixel (e-reading) person, I don't think it really matters. Although we would encourage you to be both—variety is the spice of life, after all!

Try to expand your subject areas to expose yourself to things that you aren't typically exposed to. The merits of learning to increase your expertise might be obvious, but the merits of learning about something you don't think you want to learn about might not be as obvious. Whenever you learn about an entirely new thing, even if it is something you initially thought or are sure you don't want to learn a great deal about, several things happen. First, knowing about a lot of things makes you a more interesting person. For example, I am never going to drive a semitruck on ice, nor will I probably ever meet someone who does, but I have watched *Ice Road Truckers* on the History Channel. Does this show fit in with what I typically watch and/or am interested in? No. Which is precisely why I sat down and watched it. To learn.

This same idea applies to events and activities. If you always do what you always do, you'll always be the same. Not that you aren't amazing already, of course, but staying the same is not what humans are supposed to do. We are supposed to change and evolve—that's how we grow!

Formal Learning

Workshops and Webinars

Workshops and webinars are wonderful—the "one and done" aspects of these types of formal learning experiences make it easy to fit these into even the busiest of lives. In the interest of full disclosure, we do offer webinars and also conduct workshops—www.brandchicks.com—so this advice might seem slightly biased, but you will just have to trust us that (1) we loved these things prior to doing them ourselves and (2) even though we offer them we still attend LOTS of other workshops and webinars conducted by others.

While you will probably never be able to attend all of the workshops or watch all of the webinars you would like, it is also easy not to attend any because you are always "too busy." So we recommend giving yourself a quota—whatever makes sense for you: one a month? Two every six months? One a week? It doesn't matter what the quota is, as long as you are doing something every so often, and that the quota makes sense to you—AND (most importantly) that you meet it!

Note: Many employers will pay for workshops and webinars and other learning opportunities, so be sure to research this. You wouldn't turn down free learning, would you?

Conferences

Conferences are really important to both your informal learning and your professional growth. Not only can you listen to speakers and attend sessions, you can meet others in your industry and network with those who are also moving up in their fields. Conference folks are just about always good folks to meet. Very few people who attend conferences are not "going places." Research conferences being hosted by the premiere trade group in your industry. Ask people, "What are the best conferences to go to?" Find the one(s) that offer the most "bang for their buck" as far as programming and networking opportunities (and conferences are typically held in nice places, so that is a bonus!).

Sometimes your employer will pay for you to attend your industry conference, which of course is amazing and we fully support all activity of this kind. But sometimes (or often or always) you may have to pay your way yourself. Don't get into the "I shouldn't have to pay for work stuff myself" mind-set, as this—pardon the frankness of this next comment—is the talk of losers! Investing in yourself and your career (and perhaps even your personal life) by attending conferences is just about always money well spent.

How to Master Your Next Conference

Now that you are registered for a conference, it's time to talk about mastering it. You (or your employer) have paid good money for you to attend, and you are using days of YOUR life to do so. Therefore, let's make it count!

1. Make a plan. Look at the conference materials ahead of time to decide which activities and sessions will be best for you. Are there extra things you are interested in (lunches, dinners, "field trips," etc.)? Don't wait until the last minute to sign up for them as some things sell out (and there really is no excuse for missing something for that reason!). Also consider whether there are family or friends you want to see during your trip. Are there professional colleagues you might like to see? If so, contact them ahead of time and make your visits work for YOUR schedule. Anything that's important for you to do, make a plan to do it. However, be sure to schedule some time each day to relax or take advantage of an opportunity that you didn't know about ahead of time (an impromptu invitation from a new friend or colleague is what most typically comes up!).

2. Figure out your wardrobe. Simple, easy-to-travel-with clothing is best for conferences. If you need to get something professionally cleaned, make it happen. For me, I usually bring a few pairs of black pants and a variety of solid-colored tops with black jackets or sweaters (depending on the weather). I also try to bring just a few pairs of cute-but-comfortable shoes, and jewelry that I can wear with more than one outfit. (In fact, often I'll wear the same jewelry for the entire conference.)

3. Give yourself quotas. Just like with workshops and webinars (above), give yourself a quota. I will meet ____ new people each day. Or I will visit ____ of booths. Or I will pass out ____ business cards. Giving yourself quotas encourages you to "get out there."

4. Allow for flexibility or "I've had enough!" breaks, if you need them. Conferences can be so packed with activities and so overwhelming that you might need some "alone" time or need a break every once in a while in order to be your most fabulous self while meeting all of these new people. Look at the conference schedule for possible opportunities to take a step back if you need it. If you don't need it when it comes, great. If you do—take advantage!

Is Graduate School for You?

This is a tough question for many people. For some, it's an automatic "yes," but for most the answer is "maybe." Let us help you get off the "maybe train" and make a concrete and appropriate decision for YOU.

Note: Thank you to my Fresno State colleagues, Dr. Katherine Adams and Dr. Kelley Campos McCoy, for their thoughtful input in this section!

Not-So-Good Reasons to Go to Graduate School

If any of the following are among your thoughts, perhaps you should think a little more.

- I'm bored.

- I have nothing else to do.

- I didn't get a job yet, so . . .

- I need a way to kill time before I . . .

- It would be really cool if people called me "Doctor . . ."

People have been successful in graduate school that have gone for the above reasons, but many more have dropped out if those were their primary motivations. Why? Graduate school is HARD. It's a whole different ballgame from your undergraduate degree, which may have been difficult also, but the rigor is what separates graduate school from "phase 1" of your college experience.

That said, "hard" does NOT equal "impossible." "Hard" does equal that you have to WANT it. If you don't really want it, don't do it. No one has time and money to waste.

Ponder Your Career Goals

There are some fields that require a master's degree (or a doctorate) and, therefore, if you want to get into or move forward in those fields, your choice is obvious. You have to get an advanced degree. If this is you, skip the next few sections and pick up this chapter again when it comes to choosing the right school and being successful when you get there!

A Story

In David's field, civil engineering, the prevailing thought is that having a master's can be considered a plus, but rather than spend years on a doctorate, most employers want to see those years spent gaining real-world experience. In many cases, real-world experience trumps a doctorate to an employer looking to hire. Also, in his field (and many others), there are certain professional licenses one can obtain. These licenses represent a major milestone and accomplishment for an individual's career, and in order to qualify for the license, certain parameters must be met. These parameters weigh heavily toward real-world experience, almost completely negating the value of a doctorate. So in this case and others like it, the years spent gaining a degree instead of gaining working experience can actually hurt you in the long run. This applies to civil engineers, geologists, surveyors, and many other professionals. While it is true that having a doctorate is still a major accomplishment, the "industry standard" is to get the license first. If after that you feel the need to obtain an additional master's/doctorate, if it could be used to strengthen your career goals, THEN it's OK.

If you have a choice (meaning that you can succeed just fine without an advanced degree in your field), then you have a less obvious decision. We can help you make it. Read on.

Envision the Future You

When you think about yourself in the future—what do you see? Is a master's degree important to your vision of yourself? Is it something you've always wanted? Will an advanced degree bring you large amounts of satisfaction and pride? Just "wanting" it is plenty enough reason in our opinion—even if it won't directly advance your career goals.

I counsel students all the time about whether or not (and when) they should continue their education. In our industry (public relations), it is not a huge career advantage to have a master's degree. It's LOVELY, of course, and a master's degree is always a GOOD thing on your resume, but it is not a necessary requirement for advancement in public relations. So when I counsel students, my first question is always the same, "Do you want to get a master's degree?" If the answer is anything close to "no" or "I don't know," I advise them to (at the very least) wait.

Assess How You Feel about School

Do you love school? Is learning fun? Is the end of summer/beginning of fall (aka "back-to-school") your favorite time of year? If so, you are probably the type of person who would enjoy graduate school. Pursuing an advanced degree is an intellectual pursuit, and if you don't like to learn new things, or you hate teachers, or exams, or papers, or research, then you aren't going to want to go to graduate school. While these things sound obvious to most people, I have counseled many people who haven't considered these things.

If the thought of going back to school makes you happy and excited, then you are on the right path. However, even if you were not a "back-to-school" nerd like I was (and still am!), if you enjoyed your undergraduate degree and the idea of a more focused, individualized learning experience interests you—read on!

Consider the Timing

Please understand that there is no perfect time to go to graduate school (or, frankly, for anything else that is major in your life). There will always be something that "isn't quite right." This is something you'll need to work through. If you are waiting for the perfect time, you might end up waiting forever. And waiting forever doesn't get you anywhere.

A Story

I attended graduate school at Fresno State from spring 1995 to spring 1999. In May 1997 I had my first child, so I was either pregnant or taking care of a newborn during most of this time. Was this ideal timing? Obviously not. Would I change anything? Nope. This was the "when" for me, and that is the lesson of this section. I chose to go to graduate school knowing that I would probably be pregnant during this time for two reasons: (1) I had decided on my career goal—teaching at the college level—and I had to have a graduate degree to achieve my goal; and (2) I knew that once I started my master's degree program, because of my personality, I would most certainly finish, regardless of what happened in between and how long it took me.

To add to the craziness of this story, I'll share the two most vivid memories of graduate school. One is waddling (literally) across the campus to class because in order to find a parking spot I always had to park at the complete opposite end of campus from where I needed to be. The other memory is walking up the stairs holding my two-week-old daughter with my mom behind me carrying the stroller, as the elevator was not working. I had to turn in a paper, and there was no stopping me! (Thanks again, Mom!)

Assess Your Available Time

Because the timing will never be perfect for you to get your master's and/or doctorate degree, giving some thought to your available time is extremely important to the "when" piece of this puzzle. You may have noticed that in the above story that I went to graduate school while I was pregnant with my FIRST child. There is not a chance in you-know-what that I could have done it while being pregnant with my second and already having a toddler.

Really evaluate whether or not you can "fit in" this amazing and fabulous challenge. Will this be your full-time pursuit, or will you need to stay working? Could you work part time or not at all? If you must work full time, could you still cut back on your hours? When will you study? Do you want to attend full or part time? How quickly do you want or need to finish? How many classes do you think you could take at a time? And given that plan, how long will it take you?

In your evaluation, "having time" should not include planning on getting four hours of sleep or getting up at 4 a.m. every day (especially if you are not a morning person). "Having time" should be realistic. So be really honest with yourself and the advantages and disadvantages of your current situation.

If you are fairly certain you have the time, and you are certain that you really want to do it—do it! If the time just isn't there even if you forced it—wait. But plan for when you will go so that you will make it happen.

Think about the Money

For most of us, graduate school is not free. (But if it is free for you— woo hoo! Go you!) So make sure that this is a good fiscal decision for you as well. (Again, this may sound obvious, but as you learned in chapter 2 most folks don't pay enough attention to their finances!) Research financing options (often employers will pay for master's degrees) and make sure that the burden will not be too great and/or debilitating once you are done. A solid cost-benefit analysis would be a prudent step here. Be sure to consider both monetary and nonmonetary costs and benefits (i.e., personal satisfactions, length of financial hardship, others your decision may affect, etc.).

Just like assessing your available time, you need to assess how much you can and are willing to invest in furthering your education.

Evaluate Your Chances of Success

Do you like to write? Are you a fan of the library? Of research? Of reading and reading and reading? If so, you are a good candidate for graduate school. If not, how severe is your dislike for these things? And could you be successful in spite of this?

Ask those whom you trust for an honest, authentic assessment of you and graduate school.

> **Note:** Don't ask me, because I won't be honest. While I'm typically a very "real" person when people ask me for advice, I have never discouraged anyone from going to graduate school, even if I wasn't quite "sold" on the person's chances for success. The reason—I believe that if you want something bad enough you will make it happen, and I don't believe I have the ability to measure "want." So my advice to you about whether or not to attend graduate school will always be "If you want it—GO FOR IT!"

What about the subject you are considering studying? Do you LOVE it? Does thinking about it make you happy? Are people in your life tired of hearing about it? Are you willing to (literally) live with it night and day for the next few years? Pause and ponder all of these things.

Should You Go to Graduate School RIGHT NOW?

There are many reasons why going right from your undergraduate program to graduate school might be the best option for you.

One advantage to going straight through is momentum. You've got the rhythm of school in your life, and you can just continue that rhythm right into graduate school without changing your lifestyle significantly. And, if you get your master's at the same university where you obtained your bachelor's degree, you will have a very small learning curve regarding the how's and where's of the campus.

Another reason to "go straight through" is speed to the finish line. Especially if an advanced degree is the only path to achieving your career goal, you need to buckle down and do it. If you go from one degree to the next, you will most certainly finish in the least amount of time.

Or Should You Work "for a While" First?

I worked in my field for four years before going back to school, so this is my frame of reference. I personally believe that working for a while benefited me tremendously in my graduate program because I had a lot of "real life" stories and experiences to share with my professors and classmates. I could compare and contrast what we were learning with my own experiences. This was fun for me. Many people agree that waiting makes the experience richer.

Another reason that I waited was because I wasn't exactly sure what I wanted to do. I knew that having a master's degree was important, but I wasn't 100 percent sure of what to study. I pondered an MBA for a while, and I also pondered a teaching credential and something in education. My lack of aptitude for high-level math steered me away from an MBA, and my extremely humbling and eye-opening experience as a substitute teacher led me away from pursuing a career in elementary education.

If you aren't sure, waiting is good, as often the answer will come to you if you give it time.

A Story

My "light bulb" moment came when I was speaking to a group of government safety officers about a program I was working on. It was so much fun, and the audience was so responsive, that I decided right then and there that I was, in fact, destined to be a teacher. I was just meant to be a teacher of adults, not little children. Bam! Plan formulated. All I had to do after that was implement my plan.

Another reason to wait is deceptively simple—to give you a "break" from school. Regardless of whether or not you juggled three jobs or other responsibilities during your undergraduate experience, most would agree that college is a bit of a grind. There is a lot of work and pressure, and it can be both physically and mentally exhausting. And you might need or want a break. Not a bad reason to wait, and I, in fact, think it's a good one. Another question I ask my students pondering graduate school is "How sick of school are you?" If the answer is "not at all"—I encourage them to keep pondering. If they make a disgusted face, I encourage them to wait.

Saving up money, deciding on your "real" career path, traveling and "doing something else for a while" are all completely fine reasons for waiting a bit before taking the plunge.

As you have read in this book, your ultimate success is all about what works for YOU and YOUR LIFE—not anyone else's.

WHERE Should You Attend Graduate School?

This may or may not be a big question for you. If you want/need to attend graduate school in or near the city where you live right now, your choices will probably be very few. If this is the case, evaluate each program (its size, available courses, faculty, student population, cost, etc.) and then make the best choice for you.

> **Tip:** I have found that the most interesting and exciting learning comes from being with people who are different from you. Whether the differences are in race or ethnicity or age or socioeconomic status or family makeup or religion, having the opportunity to hear from someone who is looking at things from a different perspective is truly a gift. I encourage you to consider this as you are deciding on a school. If everyone in your classroom is the same, the opportunity for growth is smaller.

If you can go anywhere, things are a little more complicated (and, some might argue, more fun!). Whatever process you used to decide on where to receive your undergraduate education might be helpful here as well. Think about the things you chose to ponder when making that decision, and see if they would be good things to ponder with this decision as well. A lot has changed since then, we know, but you made a good choice the first time (we hope), so you might want to consider a similar decision-making process.

One thing to consider is where you want to launch at least the first part of your postgraduate school career. As you recall from your undergraduate experience (especially if you have read our first book, *Land Your Dream Career: 11 Steps to Take in College*), you can and should obtain a lot of contacts in the region where you attend college. And contacts are one of the best ways to get jobs, so the more contacts you have in a region the easier it will be to get a job in that region.

Think about what kind of experience you want to have. Do you want to attend a school that is more focused on a specific career or industry, or one that is focused more on research and leads to a doctoral program? Does a commuter school work best for you, or do you want to be part of a university community where many of your fellow students live on or near campus?

What about the faculty? Do they share your interests? Read their work and imagine if you would enjoy working on similar projects.

Will you want to work on campus as a graduate assistant or teaching assistant? Are those opportunities available?

Another thing to consider is moving and travel costs. Will you want to visit your family often? How feasible will that be? How will you get your stuff to your new home?

And, you'll want to consider the weather. Is there rain or snow or heat that you aren't used to? Don't underestimate weather as an important factor in life satisfaction. There are people who are just fine in one-hundred-plus-degree weather and some that are beyond miserable in that same climate. The same goes for tons of rain or snow. Make sure you research EVERYTHING about your potential new home.

If at all possible, try and go to a different university from where you obtained your bachelor's degree. In education, change is almost always good. Especially if you are getting your advanced degree in the same subject, it will serve you well to learn from new instructors and have new classmates and learn in a new environment.

Note: I realize that this advice might sound hypocritical to you if you know that I received both my bachelor's and master's degree at the same place. This was a life and family necessity for me. To prove how much I value this idea, I will share with you that this is the advice I give to MY students—especially when our department had a graduate program. And this is also why I encourage my students—as much as I adore them—to not take all of their classes from me. Diversity of perspective is essential to a solid education.

What about Online Degrees?

By the time this book is published, there will be even more online options available to you for all kinds of degrees, and you may want to explore some of them. Or you may not. I'm hopeful that it is obvious to you that a fully online degree is a very different experience than an in-person or even a hybrid program (where some of your courses are online and some are in a traditional classroom). I encourage you to think about all of your options and chose the one that is best for *you*.

I will, however, try to persuade you not to go for a fully online degree. The reason is simple—there is more to college (at all levels) than the subject-specific knowledge you obtain. That is your primary reason for getting the degree, I understand, but you might miss the rest of it in an online program. The people piece is the most significant—both with your classmates and your instructors. These people have the opportunity to be lifelong mentors and friends if you have the chance to spend time together in the same room. Sitting in the desk next to someone is a very different social experience than being in a chat room with them as you sit at your laptops in your respective kitchens. It's both the verbal and the nonverbal aspects of communication that lead to full and deep connections. Online learning tends to be void of "small talk" and "chit chat" and even tangents that can lead to laughter and connection and even more significant learning.

The other piece missing from fully online learning is the "added value" component—the other things—not subject related—that you can and do learn from your instructors and classmates either through observation or additional conversations and connections. There is no way to measure this value, but I would argue that on many occasions it is priceless.

Talk to Those Who Have "Been Through It"

Visit with as many people as you can—just a few minutes is all you need. Ask current and former students, professors, administrators, and others these questions: (1) What are the best parts of this program? (2) What are its challenges? (3) Would you make the choice to come here again? (4) Would you recommend this program to your children?

If you can, attend an academic conference in your discipline and talk to the graduate students there. As you talk to students who are at the school you are considering, think about whether you could see yourself working with them.

Visit campuses if you can. Each campus has its own personality, and you want to make sure your choice matches or complements you! If you can't visit campuses, talking to people via Skype or a similar service is a great way to get more information than you can via a phone call or email conversation. If possible, the person you are talking to can even use his/her webcam to "show you" parts of the campus!

Don't Worry about Program Titles

As you explore programs, don't worry at all about what a program is called. Academics (and I can say this because I am one of them) get a little crazy sometimes when it comes to naming programs. And sometimes a program is called something but the content is something entirely different. Look at the names and descriptions of the COURSES. This is where you will get a feel for what you'll be learning. If, as you are reading, you want to take all of the classes RIGHT NOW, you know you are on the right track.

Trust Yourself

The bottom line is to trust yourself. As you explore different programs, some of them should "feel" right to you. These are the programs you should look at seriously. If your "gut" tells you it's not a match—you guessed it—it's not a match!

How to Succeed in Graduate School

If you choose to get a graduate degree, we (of course) want you to be successful. So here are some tips for increasing your chances of success:

Note: Thank you to the following amazing people for their ideas and advice for this section: Jules Bounchareune, Abrie Denning, Tracy Edwards, Nate Goyer, Alyssa Jarrett, Alisa Manjarrez, Jessica Medina, Dr. Don Simmons, Cassidy Smith, and Dr. Doug Swanson.

Study at Work (on Breaks, of Course!)

I did the majority of my thesis work during my lunch breaks, and I know many other people who worked full time while going to school who did the same thing. Coming in early and staying late to study at work is also helpful, as sometimes being away from home is the only way to get things done as you tend to be more focused! This is especially true if you have a family or roommates who (understandably) want or need your attention when you are at home. Set up a schedule, and stick to it!

Make Your "Work" Work for You

If at all possible, try to make your class projects, papers, and thesis sync with what you are already doing in your workplace—or what you'd like to do upon graduation. This is such a win-win as you are able to merge your worlds. This makes your life easier and also provides valuable information for your employer.

Hang in There

Graduate school is not easy, and your path will most likely not be smooth. Don't give up. If this is important to you, find a way to keep going. You might not finish as fast as you initially thought you would, or you might not end up doing the exact work that you originally set out to do, but you will do it if you keep going. It's a marathon, not a sprint, and there is nothing terribly smooth about marathons.

I am a huge San Francisco Giants fan, and one of their announcers, Mike Krukow, always says "that was a Big League hang-with-it" when someone has a long or challenging at-bat. This is what you will need in the middle of graduate school—a Big League hang-with-it—meaning that you'll need to stick with it when the going gets tough. And you can do it!

Join Forces

You might want to create your own group (or *cohort* to use a term very popular with graduate programs) of fellow graduate students (not necessarily even in your program) to support each other, work together, whine, laugh, and—of course—celebrate! No one quite understands the experience of graduate school like those who are going through it themselves. I completely agree! You can also have group study sessions and help each other every step of the way.

Don't Forget What You Learned in Chapter 4

Taking care of yourself is important no matter what you do, but if you are going to take on the extra responsibilities associated with graduate school, this is especially important. Take the time to make sure you are "operating on all cylinders" so you can have the stamina to not only persevere but also enjoy the process. Get enough sleep, eat nutritiously, and find some way to manage the stress that comes from the higher level of rigor and expectations of getting a master's and/or doctorate degree. Make a schedule for both work and play. You need down time. No one can be productive 24/7. Even you.

Use Some Vacation

You might have to take a half-day or whole day off from your job every once in a while (perhaps as finals near) to "get it all done." There is no shame in this—you are not a superhero! And while you might not be thrilled with this "use" of your paid or unpaid time off, you need to do what you need to do. If you are facing a full day of work and then eight hours of studying on top of that—choose a different plan!

Work Well with Your Peers

As an undergraduate, you were probably just like my students who tell me that group work is their least favorite part of their classes. As a graduate student, you probably will feel the same way (at least a little). Group projects are challenging, especially when you are not located in the same office (or even the same city) and have different schedules and work habits and sleep patterns and favorite ways to communicate.

Working in teams is most successful when the expectations are clear from the beginning. Have a shared vision of what success looks like, and make sure everyone can articulate that vision. This shared vision will help the group focus on what does and does not need to be done and make everyone more efficient. The group leader should continually "beat the drum" of this vision to keep everyone on track. The vision should be the litmus test for measuring priorities and setting meeting agendas.

Work Well with Your Professors

Here's a secret about professors: We really aren't all that hard to figure out. We give students clues daily regarding what our pet peeves are, what is important to us, and more. And, if we don't, we are over the moon with happiness if a student asks us to reveal this information. Read your syllabi thoroughly. Look at the percentage of points attributed to the assignments, papers, and exams and you'll have a great deal of information regarding what your priorities should be and what is important to your professor. When you get a new assignment, ask what the professor's vision of an "A" would be on that assignment. Many clues will be revealed, I promise you!

Offer to help your professors with their projects; this helps you get to know them better! Or, offer an idea for a project that you think you would both benefit from working on. Be creative! Perhaps even brainstorm together!

A Story

As you know, I went to graduate school for the primary purpose of becoming a college professor. In order to get some experience, I offered to do an independent study with one of my professors. I pitched the idea that I would study best teaching practices in public relations and then try some of them in his classroom and evaluate the results. I was able to "teach" his class once a week, try some creative things, and really learn a lot. This was great for everyone— my professor got some help in the classroom, I got some teaching experience, and the students got some new ideas and activities that they wouldn't have otherwise been exposed to.

Remember that your professors might turn into wonderful mentors as well as job references—something we all need more of! While I share job opportunities with all of my students, I sometimes will be able to match my "stars" with their ideal jobs simply because I know them better through our work together. And, because I am only one person, I can't mentor all of my students in depth, but I am able to mentor those who I work with on projects. Hopefully you will use this knowledge as additional incentive to really put effort in continuing relationships with your college faculty that can benefit you (and them!) in a myriad of ways.

Focus Your Work

As much as you can, use every assignment and paper to complete work toward your thesis or culminating project. At the very least, try to have most of your work in the same general research area. As tempting as it is to explore different things, your path to finish is much smoother when you use each research opportunity as a chance to dig further into your main research agenda. This way you won't be doing a brand-new-from-scratch literature review when it comes time to "really start" your thesis or project. You'll have a huge jump on it because you have been working on it all along. I was given this advice and didn't follow it for my first year, unfortunately. I saw how much I could benefit from using it and switched to this plan for the rest of my time in graduate school.

Get Buy-In from Those Closest to You

I don't want to say that you will not be successful in graduate school if your spouse/family/significant other doesn't support you. But I will say that this will make your life extremely and, frankly, unnecessarily challenging. Have very blunt and honest discussions with those closest to you and let them know that you will have less time for them during this process—and that you need them to help you. Perhaps set up regular "study hours" when it's best if you are not interrupted. If you explain that fewer interruptions means that you will get done faster, this might encourage them to respect your "study hours" a little more.

That said, make sure that you don't ignore these people completely, or they might not be there for you when you are finished. Make time for them, and make sure you are "present" during this time. I read an article about Kyra Sedgwick in *MORE* magazine in which she talked about a mantra that was something like "have your heart where your feet are," meaning that it is important to "be" where your feet are. If you are studying, don't be worried that you aren't with your loved one(s). If you are with your loved one(s), don't be worried about studying (or work or cleaning or whatever else). This is amazing advice that we all should heed!

Many colleges will provide an introduction to the "life of a student" during their studies, and these are both for enrolling students as well as their families. Inviting your partner/spouse/significant other to these sessions will provide a direct understanding of what life will be like during graduate school for you and those closest to you. This way your partner can prepare himself/herself for taking this additional workload on, and also understand the mind-set of you as a student. (This knowledge is especially handy during stressful times like exams and midterms.)

Have your partner go with you to school occasionally and make friends with your classmates. This can help avoid an "us and them" mentality (i.e., "You are studying, I am at home"). If your partner can participate, and perhaps even audit a course here and there, he/she can have direct interaction with others and be able to appreciate the situation from your perspective. Your partner could even join in on the discussion, enriching all parties involved!

Please also make time NOT to study. Arrange for certain nights to be "no books night" and focus on your partner and his/her needs. Life and relationships are all about balance, and if you help your partner feel appreciated and heard, this will enable you to feel better and even focus more when it comes time to study. It's all about the ebb and flow.

Anticipate the Unexpected

Don't wait until the last minute. Your time tends to be even more valuable in graduate school, and wiggle room tends to be rare. Having to make time to get a new printer cartridge (or paper), or taking a sick parent or child to the doctor, can really hamper your ability to make a deadline. Set yourself up for success by shooting for getting things done ahead of time, and then you have time to manage the things that you weren't expecting to manage.

CHEAT SHEET

- Informal learning
  - Be open
  - Observe
  - Collect smart people
  - Surf the Web
  - Read offline

- Formal learning
  - Workshops and webinars
  - Conferences
  - How to master your next conference

- Is graduate school for you?
  - Not-so-good reasons to go to graduate school
  - Ponder your career goals
  - Envision the future you
  - Assess how you feel about school
  - Consider the timing
  - Assess your available time
  - Think about the money
  - Evaluate your chances of success
  - Should you go to graduate school right now?
  - Or should you work "for a while" first?

- o Where should you attend graduate school?
- o What about online degrees?
- o Talk to those who have "been through it"
- o Don't worry about program titles
- o Trust yourself

- How to succeed in graduate school
  - o Study at work (on breaks, of course!)
  - o Make your "work" work for you
  - o Hang in there
  - o Join forces
  - o Don't forget what you learned in chapter 4
  - o Use some vacation
  - o Work well with your peers
  - o Work well with your professors
  - o Focus your work
  - o Get buy-in from those closest to you
  - o Anticipate the unexpected

CHAPTER TEN
SET YOURSELF UP FOR SUCCESS
Betsy

C ongratulations! You are well on your way to a successful, fabulous life that is exactly what YOU want! We are thrilled and honored that you chose to read our book, and we have an amazing amount of confidence in your ability to put all of this advice into practice. This chapter puts a bow on the rest of the book, allowing you to adopt a mind-set that we are certain will propel you forward (whatever forward means to YOU!) every single day. We will share more tips and strategies for getting the life that you want as you transition from college student to professional.

Note: Thank you to these great folks for ideas that helped with this chapter: Stephanie Carter, Jeff Chavez, Dani Hendricks, Shelly King, Tanya Osegueda, Jeanette Urquizo, and Jill Wagner.

But first, I must make a confession.

When I sat down to begin work on this chapter, I was experiencing a week in which I had NOT been setting myself up for success. I had been late to a couple of appointments, forgotten to bring things that I needed throughout my day, and I hadn't cooked dinner in about three days. These are classic symptoms of someone who is doing the opposite of the title of this chapter.

I am sharing this with you not to undermine my credibility, but to remind us all that setting yourself up for success is a practice, much like yoga or playing an instrument. We believe that most things exist on a continuum, and this idea is no different. As you go through your life there will be times when you are really great at this, and times that you are horrible, but most of the time you'll be somewhere in between. The more you use the tips and tricks in this book, the closer you will be to the "on it" end of the continuum!

I could also tell I was struggling because I had spent the last few days feeling as if I wasn't doing ENOUGH. I wasn't spending enough time with my family, wasn't eating enough healthy foods, wasn't exercising enough, wasn't being productive enough at work . . . you may have experienced this! When you are having an "I'm not doing enough" period, that is a big-humongous-fairly-serious clue that you need to STOP and REGROUP. That is what I did to get me rolling on this chapter, and what we want you to do every time you feel "out of control" or "not quite in sync" with your life.

> **Note:** When, a few weeks after writing this chapter's first draft, I went back to edit and finish, I felt so differently, and very solidly in control, that I actually considered deleting the above paragraphs. But I decided to keep them, and this one, as I think this is the whole point. Your life is ever changing, and you want to make sure you have tools to keep you on track throughout those changes.

Here is the blueprint for stopping and regrouping, which is the key to setting yourself up for success. It shouldn't surprise you that the blueprint for setting yourself up for success looks very similar to the contents section of this book. As you have learned in the previous chapters, you need to look at all areas of your life in order to make the life you want. It's not just about work or just about home, it's about all of it.

Establish Daily Benchmarks

In order to set yourself up for success, you need to decide what success looks like. What's interesting (or frustrating, depending on your personality), is that your definition of success will probably be different every day, week, month, season (or even every hour depending on how things are going!).

Let's start small—for tomorrow, what does success look like? Establish benchmarks in your key life areas:

- What does success look like tomorrow re: your health?

- Re: your friends/family?

- Re: your job?

- Re: your hobbies?

- Re: the other areas of your life that are important to you?

You answer these questions by pausing and pondering (there is that idea again!) and envisioning yourself at the end of tomorrow and what you will need to accomplish in order for you to deem yourself as "successful" for the day.

When doing this exercise, you will want to keep in mind your available time, energy, and resources. Also, some days you might not do anything in one or more of your LIFE PRIORITIES, and if you "plan" for this ahead of time, you can decide that this is OK, enabling you to increase your satisfaction with both your life and yourself. There is little that is more stress producing than feeling as if you aren't accomplishing what you believe you need to be accomplishing. If you purposefully (either actually or metaphorically) mark some categories/tasks "off your list," you won't feel guilty about neglecting them.

Once you have established your success benchmarks, you can create a plan of attack. The more realistic and feasible your plan, the higher the odds of it being fully implemented. As you recall, chapter 1 is full of strategies and plans for using your time to your biggest benefit. Feel free to review either the full chapter or the cheat sheet at the end of the chapter any time you need a "boost" in this area.

Of course, at the end of each day, you should circle back to your benchmarks and do a little evaluation. How did the day go? Did you do what you set out to do? Why not? Were you too ambitious with your plans? Not ambitious enough? Were other people's priorities a challenge for your priorities?

A question we insist you ask yourself each evening is this one: "Did you enjoy your day?" Every day is not going to be fabulous, but most days really should be if the way you spend your time is aligned with your LIFE PRIORITIES. Please pay attention to the answer to this question. If you see a negative pattern here—consider it as a red flag and an invitation to do some serious adjustments!

There are many other ways to set yourself up for success. Let's explore some more of them.

Set Up Your Physical Spaces

Setting up your physical spaces is critical for setting yourself up for success. Having what you need where you need it is essential for the busy professional if he/she is going to reach his/her goals. The more you set up your physical spaces to help you be successful, the more time you'll have to do what you want to do. Pause for a moment, and think about the people that you know whose houses or offices or cars are a cluttered disaster. Usually these are the same people who struggle with accomplishing their goals. Coincidence? We don't think so. There is a STRONG correlation between physical clutter and mental clutter. (An extreme example is that TV show *Hoarders*.)

Setting up your physical spaces can also help you procrastinate less, as running unnecessary errands is a surefire way to procrastinate—something I'm sure you are already aware of.

Think of the physical spaces you need to live your life—your desk, your car, your kitchen, your apartment/house. What do you need to have in each of these places in order to do what you need to do? Here is a list of action items to get you started, and some suggestions to help you out. (We are sure you'll think of more!)

Yard

- Pull all the weeds and make a plan so they will stay pulled.

- Water and mow on a regular basis.

- Include something that you find beautiful (a plant, a wind chime, a flower, a tree—what it is doesn't matter as long as you find it beautiful).

- Sit outside for a few minutes at least a few times a week (in both your front yard and backyard) so you can appreciate your work and be inspired to continue. When people don't spend time in their yards, the yards tend to get neglected. At the very least, keep your blinds/windows open so you can look out at it. (If you find yourself closing blinds so you don't have to see the mess that is your yard, it's time to clean it up!)

Entryway

- Put the items you need to take with you tomorrow morning near the door.

- Put the items you need to return to others all in the same place, and make it a habit to check that space as you are gathering your items for tomorrow.

Kitchen

- Plan your meals for the week and buy what you need to fix them.

- Organize your fridge, freezer, and your pantry so you can see what you have so you don't buy things unnecessarily and you can find things more easily.

Bedroom

- Have a place for dirty clothes that is not a chair or an unused piece of exercise equipment.

- Get rid of all clutter. Where you sleep should be your sanctuary.

- Put all electronic devices in other rooms to charge. Having these items in your bedroom is typically too tempting for people; they can't resist picking them up and "just checking one thing." The life you want will not happen if you spend the beginning and end of your day glued to your phone or tablet.

These things should be part of your life, not your whole life, and having them "sleep" in the other room helps with this tremendously.

Closet

- Particularly if mornings are stressful to you, and/or you sometimes struggle with the "what should I wear" question, consider spending a few minutes the night before deciding on an outfit (or two potential outfits, if you are one who likes to feel "in the moment"). Please check the weather report before you plan (one of our favorite things about smartphones!). It doesn't set you up for success to not know that it will be one-hundred-plus degrees or raining tomorrow.

- Organize your closet so things are easy to find. Perhaps put work clothes in one area and "play clothes" in another. Organize your shoes the same way.

Bathroom

- Put your razor in the shower.

- Have extras of things like shampoo, soap, and contact cleaning solution so that if you run out it's not a crisis that throws off your whole day.

- I use plastic tubs with all of the products I use in them so I don't have anything cluttering my bathroom counter. I simply pull out the tub from underneath the sink, use everything to get ready, and then put it back underneath the sink. Everything is in one place so I can find it easily, and it also stores out of sight!

Office

- Put things where they make sense for you.

- Keep the top of your desk as clean as possible. Remember, physical clutter leads to mental clutter!

- Make sure you have all of the supplies that you need—ink, paper, pens, stapler (with staples in it), tape, paper clips, and other items.

- Refer back to chapter 6 for more tips on managing your workspace.

Car

- Make sure you have enough gas to get you where you want to go. Stopping to get gas when you weren't planning on it is a really big stress builder.

- Keep coupon books in your car so you will actually use them.

- If you live where it gets hot in the summer, keep a towel in your backseat to toss over your steering wheel to keep it from burning your hand when you get back in the car.

- If you park outside, like I do, and it gets very cold in the winter where you live, put a towel on your front and back windows to prevent them from freezing. For frosted-over windows, use cold water, not hot, as the sudden temperature change can actually cause your window to crack! Sure it takes longer to defrost, but it can save you hundreds in unnecessary repairs.

- Keep your vehicle maintained so car trouble won't interfere with your success. Being late or not showing up at all are certain brand killers! And we want you to be safe, so a well-maintained car is a good bet for safety.

- Keep it reasonably clean. When you arrive at home for the evening, take all of the garbage out of it and throw it away. If physical clutter leads to mental clutter, imagine what being around physical garbage leads to! Wash and vacuum your car frequently as well. This will give you a big mental boost and prevent embarrassment when you need to give a friend or your boss or someone a ride. (You won't have to make some lame excuse for why your car isn't clean.)

- Keep your car presentable. If you pull up to a meeting or an interview in a dirty, cluttered car, odds are that will be your first impression—one you've unknowingly given and are probably not excited about!

Be Nice to Yourself

This may be weird advice, but we encourage you to really chew on it for a minute. Many of us are much too hard on ourselves, much harder and meaner than we would ever be to another person. Be your own BFF (best friend forever). Next time you find your "self-talk" getting harsh, ask yourself, "Would I talk this way to my best friend?" If the answer is no, and it probably is, then stop and try again. While this may sound obvious, it is worth mentioning that constantly putting yourself down (either in your head or in public) and berating yourself (either in your head or in front of others) is the EXACT OPPOSITE of setting yourself up for success.

Get Up Earlier

We know we have mentioned this before, but it's worth repeating. If you get up earlier, you'll rush less, which enables you to start your day calmly. A calm start sets you up for success. A harried start does not.

Getting up earlier also enables you to accomplish more and manage your time better. At the writing of this chapter, I'm waking up at 4:55 a.m. to take my daughter to swimming practice, and then I start my day. This is extremely early, in my opinion, but if I can resist the urge to take her and then come home and crawl back into bed (which I have done a couple of times, I must admit), I always have a more productive, enjoyable, calm day.

You don't have to get up at 4:55 a.m. to get the life you want, but try getting up even thirty minutes earlier than normal for a week or two—we promise you will notice the difference!

Get Up at the Same Time Every Day

If you wake up at a different time every day, your body (and life) doesn't have a chance to get into a rhythm, or flow—something experts agree is a key component of success. Even if you get up at the same time on workdays and a different time on the weekends (as long as it is the same both weekend days), your body will adjust and thrive via these patterns. As we talked about in chapter 1, erratic sleep schedules wreak havoc on just about every area of your life—and this is NOT setting yourself up for success! Be careful when going on vacation or over three-day weekends. You can easily talk yourself into staying up late one night "because I can sleep in a bit later tomorrow," and this can snowball into a pattern that really messes with your sleep.

Manage Your Deadlines

If you are reluctant about the feasibility of this section, then you are exactly the type of person who needs to hear this message the most. Often we feel as if we are hampered by deadlines that are set by others, and sometimes we feel a lack of control over our schedule and lives. Ironically, while many deadlines that we need to meet are set by others, the deadlines leading up to meeting the deadlines are set by us, aren't they? This means that more often than not, deadline stress is not caused by others, it is caused by us.

Inappropriate or ineffective deadline management is one of the most common ways we fail to set ourselves up for success. Whether it is due to our own procrastination or our desire to give others in our lives as much time as possible to do their parts of things, poor deadline management is a surefire stress inducer, brand killer, and blood pressure riser. So, raise your right hand (seriously!) and repeat after me, "Starting today, I will use deadlines to help me set myself up for success!" (Thank you.)

One great way to get rolling with this idea is to make it a habit to build in a cushion for all of your deadlines. If you are confident you can finish something by 2 p.m., give yourself a deadline of 11 a.m. (or earlier!). That way if something that you hadn't anticipated happens (tech glitch, interruption, cool lunch invitation, etc.) you can still make your deadline (and you provide yourself with enough wiggle room to accept that lunch invitation from the cute person who works down the hall!).

Another great thought is to craft a plan whenever you are given a deadline. This doesn't have to be a long, involved thought process, but it does require some focused thinking. You can ask yourself:

- Do I understand what is required of me to complete this task? Should I ask additional questions?

- How long do I need for this task? Do I need more than one day or part of a day (morning, afternoon, evening)?

- What supplies do I need? Do I have them on hand? If not, how and when should I get them?

- Are others involved? How much time will they need?

- Does this task require drafting or editing? (Your first and second drafts shouldn't be done consecutively without any time in between.)

- Do I need new knowledge? How and when should I get it?

You can also help yourself via the deadlines you give others. Don't give other people so much time that you are rushing. That might appear obvious, but if you are honest with yourself you probably can think of a time (recently) that you gave someone more time to help them out and then ended up being stressed on your end without the appropriate amount of time to do what you need to do.

Remember the pledge you made earlier. Build in cushions all over the place, and see how deadlines become less of a burden.

Manage Your Technology

This topic has been touched upon in other chapters, but a chapter about setting yourself up for success would not be complete without a discussion about managing technology. Let's first address this very subtitle and what it means. We used the word *manage* in the title of this section very strategically. You know this, we know you do, but if you don't consciously manage your technology it will very seriously and dangerously manage you (metaphorically, of course).

Constantly monitor this aspect of your life. Ask yourself, "Am I managing my technology or is it managing me?" and "Do I feel like I am so tied to technology that I feel lost and incomplete without my [tablet, smartphone, computer, MP3 player, etc.]?" Depending on your answers, adjust! And adjust quickly!

As mentioned in chapter 1, turning off your notifications—ON EV-ERYTHING—is the best way to manage your technology. Then make a plan to "check in" with whatever you'd like to check in with, and then stick to that plan. Here is a test to determine if you are checking too frequently: If you are always getting to the bottom of your feeds, you are checking too frequently. Social media was not designed for you to consume every post from every friend, fan, or follower (unless your networks have less than ten people in them). One of the realities of engaging with social media is that there will be a lot of content that you won't be able to consume, and that is OK and essential for your success in the rest of your life.

If certain people's content is important to you, use the features of each social network to ensure that you see this content (i.e., designating people as "close friends" on Facebook, having certain tweets sent to your phone as text messages, etc.). Make habits to check and respond when others reach out to you (via direct message or @replies or likes or comments, etc.). As for the rest—enjoy what you can during the times that are engaged, and then accept the fact that you won't be able to see/read/like/favorite it all. Think of my favorite metaphor for social media—it's like drinking from a fire hose. This, by definition, makes it impossible to consume it all.

Respect the Seasons of Your Life

In order to respect the seasons of your life, you'll need to find balance in the big picture. Go back to chapter 1 and review the section on setting up your LIFE PRIORITIES. Then ask yourself how you are doing in this area. If someone followed you around for a week, would they know the things that are most important to you? This was a huge wakeup thought for me once, as I asked myself that question and the answer was absolutely not, which meant that all I was doing was giving "lip service" to ideas like balance and priorities. I was completely out of whack with how I spent my time versus what was truly important to me. You might have this happen sometimes, too, which is why it is critical to always ask yourself these types of questions.

Life is so much fun! We hope you agree, but therein lies the challenge. Because life is so much fun, it is hard to not try to do all of it at once—especially when you are twenty-something and you have boundless ideas and energy and even some available time. (Actually, it's still hard at forty-something!)

Don't Undermine Yourself

Have confidence. You are a successful adult who has already accomplished a great deal—and you are moving forward. All you need to do is keep the wheels turning and you will get there. Remember, life success is all about the compounding effect. One of my friends, Dani, likes to "pull out my WD40 spray when I feel rusty or am at a stop. I won't ever give up!"

Look for ways that you might be sabotaging your success, either consciously or unconsciously, and stop it! Are you struggling with setting up your physical spaces? Are you forgetting things because you didn't write them down? You know better—so now it's time to do better! Remember, you should at least treat yourself as well as you treat the important people in your life, and we could argue that you should perhaps even treat yourself better!

Acquire Some Patience—And Then Perhaps Acquire More Patience

In our "instant gratification" society, patience is often hard to find. We can do things so quickly via all of this fabulous technology, and we also see others accomplish their goals in what seems like an instant, and so it is hard to wait for anything anymore. But please take note the word *seems* in the previous sentence. Even if someone appears to be an overnight success, the reality is that very, very, very, very few people are actually overnight successes. And they sometimes even tell us that in interviews, ironically, talking about all the odd jobs they held and the long nights and the rejections and everything else. But because perception is reality, and we perceive them as overnight successes, in our minds that is what they are, so this is what we want as well.

A Story

When Tori and I were trying to find an agent to take on our first book, we tried for several months and had no luck initially. We received some lovely rejection letters, and even more nonresponses. It was very frustrating and discouraging, as we were pretty sure we had a book idea that people would benefit from, but we couldn't find an agent to take us on. We paused for a bit, changed the book title, and in two more weeks we got a yes from our wonderful agent, Anne. Had we given up, we wouldn't have just published our second book (this one!).

It's time for a global reality check, and time to revisit the wonderful adage "patience is a virtue." Now, this message is coming to you from someone with MAJOR issues in this area, so if you are struggling with patience, let me assure you that we could form a support group, you and I. I have joked on more than one occasion that when God was handing out patience, I was in another line. However, I have also learned and observed that when I have patience, things work out SO MUCH BETTER for me, and I'm sure you've experienced this as well.

These days, I call it "trying to be Zen" about things.

You probably aren't going to start your career making $100K, but that doesn't mean you aren't going to get there. And if the corner office is what you want, know that just because you don't start there, it doesn't mean you won't get there. If you want it, you will make it happen.

There is a terrific quote by David Bly—"Striving for success without hard work is like trying to harvest where you haven't planted." Planting takes time. But the planting can also be fun—so be sure to embrace the joy along the way!

Pause First, but Try to Say Yes

There is a delicate balance between saying "yes" too often and not saying it often enough. When we say "yes" too frequently, we end up overwhelmed and don't enjoy the things we do. However, when we say "yes" too infrequently, we find ourselves in ruts; lonely and unhappy, and perhaps still feeling overwhelmed—but in a very different way.

One of the ways to set yourself up for success regarding the perfect "saying yes ratio" is to pause first. When you evaluate whether you should say yes or no, always look for the reasons to say yes, as skewing toward the positive keeps your life going in a positive direction. Be sure to pause as you ponder (in fact, maybe make that your mantra—you can tell folks—"Hold on, I need to pause while I ponder"). Pausing while you ponder helps you listen to your gut, as you intrinsically always know whether you should say yes or no, because saying yes when you should makes you feel good, and saying yes when you shouldn't makes you feel bad. And the same goes with saying no when you should and when you shouldn't. And if your gut doesn't tell you the answer right away, pause and ponder a bit more, think about your LIFE PRIORITIES, and see if this request matches up.

Trust your first thought, but don't say your first thought out loud until you've had a chance to pause and ponder. First thoughts are helpful, as they often reveal what we really want to do, but they can also be influenced by things like social or peer pressure, fatigue, and distraction (three things that cause poor decision making!).

Try to say yes, as most people regret the things they didn't do much more than the things they did do. But also try to only say yes when the yes moves you closer to your LIFE PRIORITIES.

There Is No Perfect, but You Can Always Thrive

Things and people and experiences can be lovely, and wonderful, and horrible, and pretty-darn-close-to-perfect. But there is no perfect. And that is OK, and your life starts to be really OK once you accept this fact. Set yourself up for success by knowing that there is no perfect job, spouse, house, haircut, pet. But you can get pretty darn close, and that's what you should strive for.

And you can make the best of what you have. One of my favorite sayings is "bloom where you are planted." In fact, I have a magnet with this quote on my refrigerator. The idea here, of course, is that wherever you are, you can "bloom" (aka thrive). Usually whether we do or not is entirely up to us.

Don't Give Up

There is always more than one path to get somewhere, and if your first attempt and/or the most traditional path doesn't work, try a different one. This is perhaps an odd analogy, but this thought process reminds me of how I approach working on my computer. If my first attempt to make something doesn't work, I look for another way—a "back door" or a "work around."

This approach has worked way more times than it hasn't. I also use the approach at work, and I was even complimented recently by a colleague. She told me that she appreciated how I don't let the first roadblock prevent me from getting what I need to do done. This protocol should be your default, as it has become mine.

The first time something doesn't work, perhaps try again. If it doesn't work a second time (providing that a second try is possible) try to find the "work around." Perhaps a different person can get you the right answer. Perhaps doing the meeting on a different day of the week will solve your problem. Perhaps partnering with another organization can get you where you need to go. Perhaps doing it a completely different way will work—blow up the original model and start all over (metaphorically, of course!).

But . . . Change Course If You Need To

Whenever you find that your "work arounds" are still not getting you where you need to go, pause and ponder whether or not it is worth your time and energy to continue to move forward. We want you to practice persistence and diligence and all of those fabulous things, of course, but conversely, you should also know that changing course is sometimes the best option. Whether or not it is the best option can only be determined by you, via a very thorough cost/benefit analysis, because whether there are actual monetary costs or not, there are always opportunity costs to be considered. Often there is honor in retreat.

WOO HOO for YOU!

Please allow us to be a little "mushy" and perhaps a bit cheesy for a moment. Please don't ever forget to WOO HOO! for yourself. You've got to "believe your own hype" or none of this great advice is going to work. You are an amazing, talented, incredibly smart person. (We know this to be true because you are reading this book!) Believe that each and every day and you'll go far.

Self-doubt will find you, as it finds us all, but be sure to "kick it to the curb" as soon as you feel it trying to harm you.

Seriously. WOO HOO for YOU! You have taken the time to do something proactive for the wonderful life that you have ahead of you.

Kudos!

Final Notes

We would love to connect with you! Find us at www.BrandChicks.com where you can follow us on social media and find out more about what we are up to. At the writing of this book, we are launching a series of radio shows and webinars. And, of course, we are working on our next book!

BEST of luck in your upcoming adventures! We know you are going to be GREAT!

CHEAT SHEET

- Establish daily benchmarks

- Set up your physical spaces
  - yard
  - entryway
  - kitchen
  - bedroom
  - closet
  - bathroom
  - office
  - car

- Be nice to yourself

- Get up earlier

- Get up at the same time every day

- Manage your deadlines

- Manage your technology

- Respect the seasons of your life

- Don't undermine yourself

- Acquire some patience—and then perhaps acquire more patience

- Pause first, but try to say yes

- There is no perfect, but you can always thrive
- Don't give up
- But . . . change course if you need to
- WOO HOO! for YOU!
- Final notes

INDEX

ABOUT THE AUTHORS

Tori Randolph Terhune is an award-winning speaker, entrepreneur, and public relations and social media professional, as well as coauthor of *Land Your Dream Career: Eleven Steps to Take in College.*

Terhune's passion is to help students and young professionals succeed, which was sparked by her own college experience. By the time she walked across the graduation stage in 2009, she had three years of experience in her field and the dream job she wanted. She was recognized as the Outstanding Public Relations Graduate by Fresno State and as Rookie of the Year by the Public Relations Society of America Central California chapter.

While still a student, she published articles in newspapers and magazines, and she successfully pitched numerous print, radio, and TV stories for clients after launching her own public relations business at age nineteen. In her last semester at Fresno State, she worked with three other students to launch and operate a completely student-operated public relations firm, one of the few truly student-run firms in the nation. She served as the agency's first executive director, and the firm grew to eighteen staff members and eight clients in the first year.

Terhune has evaluated her own college-to-career experiences, as well as her peers', and perfected the best tactics to help other students succeed. She has served as a guest lecturer for public relations, ethics, writing, and entrepreneurship courses while still a student and postgraduation.

Terhune is now the chief executive officer of Brand Chicks, a company of authors, speakers, and public relations consultants from across

California who partner with individuals and companies to help them achieve branding success. By night she coaches cheerleading at Spirit Force, a nationally recognized gym, and she was awarded the Top 25 Cheer Coach in America in 2011, 2012, and 2013 by Christian Cheerleaders of America. She is a 2009 graduate of California State University, Fresno, with a degree in mass communication and journalism, with an emphasis in public relations.

Professor **Betsy A. Hays**, APR, Fellow PRSA, is a sought-after keynote speaker and workshop presenter who specializes in public relations, communication, and career topics. Her first book, coauthored with Tori Terhune, is *Land Your Dream Career: Eleven Steps to Take in College.* The book was listed in the American Library Association's Bests of 2013.

Professor Hays is the lead public relations professor for the Department of Mass Communication and Journalism at California State University, Fresno, where she has taught since 1999. In addition to managing the public relations option, Professor Hays runs the internship and scholarship programs for the department. She is also the faculty adviser for the Public Relations Student Society of America and the university's student-run PR firm, TALK.

Professor Hays earned her BA in journalism with an emphasis in public relations and her MA in mass communication from California State University, Fresno. She is also an accredited public relations professional, having earned her APR designation from the Public Relations Society of America. (The APR process is similar to an accountant becoming a CPA.) The "Fellow PRSA" designation after her name is due to being inducted into the prestigious PRSA College of Fellows in 2013.

She has been involved in the public relations profession for more than twenty-two years, having worked in the field for eight years prior to beginning her university teaching career. Professor Hays has served on the Board of Directors of the Central California Chapter of the Public Relations Society of America (PRSA) in all but two years since 1998 and was its president in 1998 and 2010. Betsy is now in her third year on the Board of Directors for PRSA's North Pacific District.

Professor Hays was named PRSA's Public Relations Professional of the Year in 2000 and has also been honored with the prestigious Provost's Award for promising new tenure-track faculty at Fresno State. She was named Outstanding Adviser at Fresno State in 2010 and Outstanding Club/Organization Adviser in 2013. Also in 2010, Professor Hays was given the Spirit of Service Award for her exemplary commitment to community engagement.

She created what is believed to be the nation's first undergraduate Public Relations Entrepreneurship courses in 2007 and is also the architect of fully integrating the pedagogy of service-learning into the university's public relations program.

Prior to her service at Fresno State, Professor Hays worked for Deen & Black Public Relations (now Ogilvy PR Worldwide) and served as both media spokesperson and media trainer for clients throughout California and Arizona, mainly in the government sector. She has also coordinated a regional public education program with sixty-two cities in Central California, helping cities spread the word about the importance of solid waste reduction. In addition, Professor Hays spent two years working in both internal and external public relations for Saint Agnes Medical Center in Fresno, California.